MacBook A

A Comprehensive Guid
2023 (with M2 Chip) Hidden Features and Useful macOS Ventura
Tips & Tricks for Both Beginners and Seniors

Perry
Hoover

Disclaimer

The information in this book is based on personal experience and anecdotal evidence. Although the author has made every attempt to achieve an accuracy of the information gathered in this book, they make no representation or warranties concerning the accuracy or completeness of the contents of this book. Your circumstances may not be suited to some illustrations in this book.

The author disclaims any liability arising directly or indirectly from the use of this book. Readers are encouraged to seek Medical. Accounting, legal, or professional help when required.

This guide is for informational purposes only, and the author does not accept any responsibilities for any liabilities resulting from the use of this information. While every attempt has been made to verify the information provided here, the author cannot assume any responsibility for errors, inaccuracies or omission.

Printed in the United States of America

Table of Contents

INTRODUCTION

During the long expected 2023 Developer's Conference, Apple surprised everyone by unveiling the 15-inch MacBook Air, which had been widely speculated about and highly anticipated. The advent of this product represents an important new step for the MacBook Air series. Along with its many other great features, the smart device is powered by the M2 Apple silicon, which gives it a fantastic battery life of up to 18 hours. The following provides information about the availability as well as the specifics of the product.

To begin, the all-new MacBook Air features an aluminum unibody construction, has a thickness of only 11.5 millimeters, and weighs only 1.4 kilograms. Notably, it is the first product to include Apple's revolutionary 15.3-inch Liquid Retina Display, which has a maximum brightness of up to 500 nits, slim bezels, and the now-iconic notch. This 15-inch MacBook Air from 2023 can boast the title of being the thinnest laptop of its size in the globe.

The speed of the 2023 MacBook Air is driven by the 2022 Apple M2 chip, which boasts an incredible configuration featuring a maximum of 10 cores for the graphics processing unit (GPU), a maximum of 8 cores for the central processing unit (CPU), a maximum of 24 GB RAM, and storage options of up to 2 TB SSD. The same pattern seen in the 2022 model is followed by this design, which includes a media engine, support for simultaneous 4K and 8K streams, a ProRes video engine, and more. In addition, the new 15-inch M2 MacBook Air released in 2023 is compatible with MagSafe charging and comes with a durable charging cable that is braided.

The headphone jack, two Thunderbolt ports, and Touch ID are all included in the 2023 MacBook Air, which also integrates them all neatly into the power button. Notable features include a 1080p Full-HD FaceTime camera that provides great video clarity and a six-speaker audio system that provides an enthralling spatial audio experience, which is enhanced by Dolby Atmos certification. Both of these systems give an exceptional audio and video experience. The product features Apple's famous Magic keyboard and a fanless, noiseless design all while being equipped with said keyboard.

Even though Apple has not announced the exact battery capacity of the MacBook Air, analysts have estimated that the device will have a battery life of up to 18 hours when playing videos. This MacBook Air is compatible with 67Wh Fast Charging, which is the same as the model that was released the year before. Midnight, Starlight, Space Gray, and Silver are the various enticing hues that are available for purchase in the portable computing device.

The all-new MacBook Air with a 15-inch display has a starting price of $1,299 (about Rs. 1,07,000), while the price for students is $1,199 (around Rs. Beginning today, pre-orders can be placed, and the product is scheduled to become available for purchase on June 13 of the year 2023.

CHAPTER ONE

New Features

Design

Apple undertook a major makeover of the MacBook Air in 2022, marking the first big overhaul since the product was first introduced in 2010. The revised MacBook Air abandoned the tapered chassis that was characteristic of earlier incarnations and instead adopted a sleek, flat-bodied design that was evocative of the MacBook Pro. The thickness of the device was kept consistent from front to back throughout the entire device.

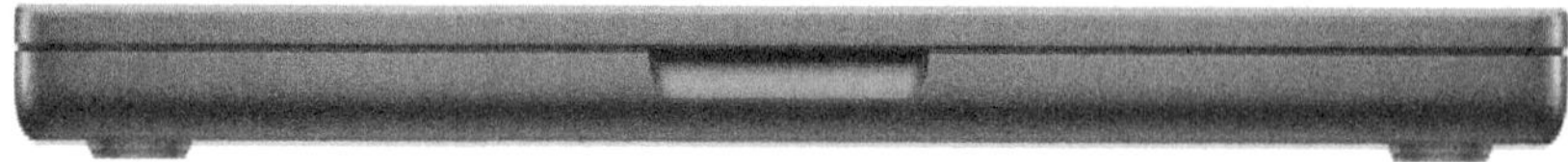

This design paradigm was continued into the year 2023 with the launch of a 15.3-inch model of the MacBook Air. This model catered to customers who were looking for a more affordable choice with a screen that was significantly larger. The 13-inch and 15-inch MacBook Air models share parallel design concepts; nonetheless, the primary differences between them are the proportions of the chassis and the size of the display.

Even though it has mostly kept the same footprint as its predecessor, the MacBook Air with a 13-inch display has a few distinguishing features. It has a profile that has a thickness of only 11.3 millimeters, which is a significant reduction from the maximum thickness of 16.1 millimeters that the previous model had. It is slightly lighter than its predecessor, which weighed 2.8 pounds, and has proportions that measure 11.97 inches in length and 8.46 inches in depth. Its weight is 2.7 pounds.

On the other hand, the MacBook Air with a 15-inch display has a significantly larger physical factor. With a measurement of 11.5 millimeters, it maintains a profile that is comparable to the elegant appearance of the 13-inch model. It has a length of 13.4 inches, a depth of 9.35 inches, and a configuration that is 3.3 pounds heavier than its predecessor.

Along with a MagSafe charging port and a 3.5mm headphone jack, both incarnations of the MacBook Air include a pair of Thunderbolt/USB-C connectors on the left side of the device. The bottom is finished with four rubber feet, which is reminiscent of the design aesthetics of the MacBook Pro.

Similar to the model from the previous generation, the display is surrounded by the same distinctive black bezels. The laptop comes equipped with a black Magic Keyboard that does not have a Touch Bar, in addition to a sizable Force Touch trackpad. In essence, it is a version of the MacBook Pro that is both smaller and lighter in weight.

You can get your hands on a MacBook Air in a variety of hues, such as silver, space gray, midnight, which is an unusual shade of deep blue, and starlight, which is a bright gold variant.

Keyboard, Trackpad, and Ports

The venerable Magic Keyboard from the previous generation of the MacBook Air has been carried over into the current model. This keyboard features a durable scissor switch mechanism that is resistant to dust and particles. This solves the problems that were caused by the outdated butterfly keyboards that were used in prior Macs.

The keyboard on the MacBook Air features a scissor mechanism, which allows for 1mm of key travel and ensures a consistent and comfortable key experience. The use of an Apple-engineered rubber dome that stores increased potential energy and improves the responsiveness of each keystroke is incorporated into the design of this product. In addition to this, the keys on the keyboard have backlighting that is controlled by an ambient light sensor. This allows the keys to be illuminated even in low-light settings.

Instead of including a Touch Bar like the M1 Pro and M1 Max MacBook Pro models do, the MacBook Air flaunts a full row of function keys as a point of differentiation between itself and those two versions.

The spacious Force Touch trackpad, which has the same layout as previous versions is hidden beneath the surface of the keyboard. This trackpad is distinguished from others in that it does not contain any conventional buttons. Instead, it is equipped with a collection of Force Sensors that provide a uniform response regardless of which part of the trackpad is pressed. When using the trackpad, users will feel a tactile response that is analogous to that of pressing a real button because it is augmented by a Taptic Engine that is powered by magnets. This takes the place of the more common tactile sensation that comes from pressing a physical button.

Touch ID

The M2 MacBook Air includes a fingerprint sensor that can be used to authenticate users using the Touch ID system. This sensor is located on the top of the keyboard, near to the function buttons. This particular implementation of Touch ID works by way of a Secure Enclave, which is a protected enclave that maintains the confidentiality of fingerprint data as well as other personal information.

When a finger is placed on the Touch ID sensor, a user is able to quickly and easily unlock their Mac, making the Touch ID feature on the MacBook Air a seamless replacement to passwords. In addition to this, it eliminates the requirement for entering passwords into apps that need to be protected, and it acts as an authentication method for conducting safe Apple Pay transactions within Safari.

The MacBook Air comes equipped with two Thunderbolt 3/USB-C connections, each of which is able to support data transfer rates of up to 40 gigabits per second. In addition to this, it has a new charging port called MagSafe 3, which is quite similar to the charging interface that was introduced in the 14- and 16-inch versions of the MacBook Pro.

Display

When comparing the displays of the MacBook Air models 2022 and 2023, we notice that there are significant variances between the two. The display on the MacBook Air 2022 measures 13.6 inches, whereas the display on the MacBook Air 2023 measures 15.3 inches, making it significantly larger than its predecessor. Both displays have thin bezels and make use of something called "Liquid Retina Display Technology." The notch on the MacBook Air is a design choice that was inspired by the one on the MacBook Pro. This choice allows for a 1080p webcam to be housed while also increasing the amount of screen real estate available.

In terms of the technical specifications of these screens, the resolution of the 13-inch MacBook Air's display is 2560 by 1664, and it offers 224 pixels per inch. On the other side, the resolution of the 15-inch MacBook Air is increased to 2880 by 1864 while keeping the same pixel density of 224 pixels per inch. The displays on both of these models support an incredible one billion different colors and come equipped with the P3 Wide color gamut, which guarantees accurate color reproduction that is vivid and true to life. These displays have a peak brightness of up to 500 nits, which helps to illuminate your visuals so that they are clear.

The incorporation of **True Tone technology** into the display of the MacBook Air is one of the characteristics that sets it apart from other displays. The color temperature of the display can be automatically adjusted by True Tone so that it is in harmony with the lighting that is present in the surrounding environment. This technology evaluates the brightness of the space as well as the color temperature. It does so with the assistance of a multi-channel ambient light sensor that is built into the MacBook Air. Using this information, the MacBook Air dynamically fine-tunes both the hue and the intensity, producing an effect that is similar to that of natural lighting settings. This not only provides you with a viewing experience that is analogous to reading from paper, but it also helps to prevent eye strain, which helps to ensure that you are comfortable even when using the device for extended periods of time.

M2 Apple Silicon Chip

Apple incorporates the M2 chip into the MacBook Air versions that measure 13.6 inches and 15.3 inches respectively. The M2, which is the successor to the M1, includes an 8-core central processing unit just like the M1. On the other hand, it supports either eight or 10 GPU cores, which is an increase from the M1's seven or eight available cores.

According to Apple's documentation, the M2 chip makes use of cutting-edge technology based on a 5-nanometer process. This incredible technological innovation improves performance per watt and incorporates a staggering 20 billion transistors, which is a 25 percent increase in comparison to its predecessor, the M1. Because of this increase in the number of transistors, the memory bandwidth has been increased to 100 gigabytes per second.

When compared, the M2 chip demonstrates significant improvements in performance. It is 1.4 times faster than the M1, and it is significantly more than 15 times faster than the previous Intel-based MacBook Air alternatives. This accomplishment was made possible by a central processing unit that is 18 percent quicker, a graphics processing unit that is 35 percent more powerful, and a neural engine that is 40 percent quicker.

The advantage of the M2 is demonstrated by benchmarks provided by Geekbench, which show an improvement of up to 20 percent in multi-core performance compared to that of the M1.

The single-core score of the M2 chip was 1919, which is a 12 percent gain over the single-core score of the M1 MacBook Air, which was 1707. The M2 chip's clock speed was 3.49GHz, in contrast to the M1 chip's clock speed of 3.2GHz. When compared to the score of 7419 achieved by the M1, the M2's multi-core score of 8928 represents an increase of 20 percent.

The M2 chip made a significant improvement in its performance when compared to the M1 chip, which only scored 21001 out of a possible 30000 points in the Metal benchmark. The highest number of cores that the M1 chip could support was eight, whereas the M2 chip offers the option of a GPU with ten cores.

In a manner analogous to that of the M1 MacBook Air, the M2-equipped machines do not utilize a fan, which results in operation that is completely silent.

In terms of memory and storage, the M2 MacBook Air is capable of supporting up to 24 gigabytes of unified memory and up to 2 terabytes of SSD storage at its absolute maximum. Memory capacities start at 8 gigabytes, and storage space is 256 gigabytes for the base versions.

Battery Life

The lithium-polymer battery in the MacBook Air with a screen size of 13 inches has a capacity of 52.6-watt hours, while the battery in the MacBook Air with a screen size of 15 inches has a capacity of 66.5-watt hours. In spite of the fact that the battery capacity of the 15-inch variant is greater, both computers are capable of delivering up to 18 hours of movie playback when utilizing the Apple TV program and up to 15 hours of wireless web browsing.

There is a 30W Dual USB-C Port Compact Power Adapter included with the standard configuration of the 13-inch MacBook Air, but there is a 35W Dual

USB-C Port Compact Power Adapter included with the enhanced configuration of the 13-inch MacBook Air with a 10-core GPU. An optional power adapter with 70W USB-C can be purchased for an additional cost of $20 if you want to take advantage of quick charging. Customers have the option of purchasing the 35W Dual USB-C Power Adapter that comes standard with the 15-inch MacBook Air basic model, but they also have the ability to upgrade to the 70W USB-C power adapter, which offers faster charging capabilities.

Other Features

Connectivity:

Wi-Fi 6, also known as 802.11ax, is supported by the MacBook Air. This standard is also known as Wi-Fi 6. The previous standard for WiFi, known as 802.11ac, has been surpassed by this new WiFi protocol in terms of both speed and efficiency. Additionally, the MacBook Air is compatible with the latest Bluetooth specification, Bluetooth 5.3, which, in comparison to the previous Bluetooth version, Bluetooth 5.0, offers increased speed and dependability.

Speakers and Microphone:

A sound system with four speakers may be found built into the MacBook Air with a 13-inch display. This improvement achieves greater stereo separation and vocal clarity by including two tweeters and two ultrathin woofers into the design of the speaker system. On the other hand, the MacBook Air with a 15-inch screen incorporates a six-speaker sound system with force-cancelling woofers, which provides an even greater degree of sound quality. This is made possible by the larger design of the 15-inch MacBook Air. Notably, the 13-inch and 15-inch models are easily distinguished from one another by virtue of their respective sound systems.

Both of the audio systems found in the different models of the MacBook Air offer support for broad wide stereo sound in addition to the cutting-edge technology known as Spatial Audio. When listening to music or watching films with Dolby Atmos on a device that has built-in speakers, the addition of Spatial Audio makes the listening experience more enjoyable. In addition, if you are using AirPods of the third generation, AirPods Pro, or AirPods Max, you have access to Spatial Audio, which includes dynamic head tracking.

The sound quality of video conversations made on a MacBook Air, which comes equipped with a three-microphone array containing directional beamforming technology, is significantly improved as a result of this technology.

FaceTime Camera:

The FaceTime HD camera on the MacBook Air is also a 1080p type, just like the one that was first introduced with the 14- and 16-inch models of the MacBook Pro in 2021. This camera is powered by a sophisticated image signal processor and is equipped with computational video capabilities, both of which significantly improve the quality of recorded video. Apple claims that this camera is superior to its predecessor in terms of performance since it has a resolution that is twice as high and performs exceptionally well in low-light settings.

Specifications

Finishes:

- Silver
- Starlight
- Space Gray
- Midnight

Processor:

- Apple M2 chip
- 8-core CPU with 4 high-performance cores and 4 energy-efficient cores
- 10-core GPU
- 16-core Neural Engine
- 100GB/s memory bandwidth
- Media engine

Video Capabilities:

- Hardware-accelerated H.264, HEVC, ProRes, and ProRes RAW
- Video decode and encode engines
- ProRes encode and decode engine

Display:

- Liquid Retina display
- 15.3-inch (diagonal) LED-backlit display with IPS technology
- Native resolution: 2880-by-1864 at 224 pixels per inch
- Brightness: 500 nits

Color:

- Support for 1 billion colors
- Wide color (P3)
- True Tone technology

Battery and Power:

- Up to 18 hours of Apple TV app movie playback
- Up to 15 hours of wireless web usage
- 66.5-watt-hour lithium-polymer battery
- 35W Dual USB-C Port Compact Power Adapter
- USB-C to MagSafe 3 Cable

- Fast-charge capable with 70W USB-C Power Adapter

Charging and Connectivity:

- MagSafe 3 charging port
- 3.5 mm headphone jack
- Two Thunderbolt / USB 4 ports with support for charging, DisplayPort, Thunderbolt 3 (up to 40Gb/s), USB 4 (up to 40Gb/s), USB 3.1 Gen 2 (up to 10Gb/s)

Memory:

- 8GB unified memory (configurable to 16GB or 24GB)

Storage:

- 256GB SSD (configurable to 512GB, 1TB, or 2TB)

Keyboard and Trackpad:

- Backlit Magic Keyboard with 78 (U.S.) or 79 (ISO) keys
- Touch ID

- Ambient light sensor
- Force Touch trackpad with pressure-sensitive capabilities

Wireless:

- Wi-Fi 6 (802.11ax)
- Bluetooth 5.3

Camera:

- 1080p FaceTime HD camera
- Advanced image signal processor with computational video

Audio:

- Six-speaker sound system with force-cancelling woofers
- Wide stereo sound
- Support for Spatial Audio with Dolby Atmos on built-in speakers
- Spatial Audio with dynamic head tracking when using compatible AirPods

Ports and Display Support:

- Simultaneous support for full native resolution and 1 billion colors on built-in display
- External display support up to 6K resolution at 60Hz
- Thunderbolt 3 digital video output
- Various output options using adapters (sold separately)

Video and Audio Playback:

- Support for HEVC, H.264, ProRes, HDR formats (Dolby Vision, HDR10, HLG)
- Audio formats: AAC, MP3, Apple Lossless, FLAC, Dolby Digital, Dolby Digital Plus, Dolby Atmos

Operating Requirements:

- Line voltage: 100V to 240V AC
- Frequency: 50Hz to 60Hz
- Operating temperature: 50° to 95° F (10° to 35° C)

- Storage temperature: –13° to 113° F (–25° to 45° C)
- Relative humidity: 0% to 90% noncondensing
- Operating altitude: tested up to 10,000 feet
- Maximum storage altitude: 15,000 feet
- Maximum shipping altitude: 35,000 feet

Size and Weight:

- Height: 0.45 inch (1.15 cm)
- Width: 13.40 inches (34.04 cm)
- Depth: 9.35 inches (23.76 cm)
- Weight: 3.3 pounds (1.51 kg)

Operating System

- **macOS**: macOS stands as the epitome of cutting-edge desktop operating systems worldwide. Unveiling its latest iteration, macOS Ventura, this platform elevates your Mac experience, enhancing productivity, unleashing entertainment possibilities, and propelling you towards unprecedented accomplishments.

Highlighted Features:

- Voice Control
- Enhance Contrast
- Switch Control
- VoiceOver
- Minimize Motion
- Magnification
- Siri and Speech-to-Text
- Live Captions

Pre-installed apps

Experience the prowess of pre-installed applications, each serving a distinct purpose in enriching your digital life. Among these tools are:

- App Store
- Books
- Calendar
- Contacts
- FaceTime
- Find My

- Freeform
- GarageBand
- Home
- iMovie
- Keynote
- Mail
- Maps
- Messages
- Music
- News
- Notes
- Numbers
- Pages
- Photo Booth
- Photos
- Podcasts
- Preview
- QuickTime Player
- Reminders
- Safari
- Shortcuts
- Siri

- Stocks
- Time Machine
- TV
- Voice Memos

The Package Contents

Your 15-inch MacBook Air package includes:

- 15-inch MacBook Air
- 35W Dual USB-C Port Compact Power Adapter
- USB-C to MagSafe 3 Cable (2 m)

Championing Environmental Responsibility

- Designed with a resolute commitment to environmental preservation, the 15-inch MacBook Air featuring the M2 chip boasts a host of eco-friendly attributes:

Exemplary Material Choices:

- Incorporation of 100% recycled aluminum in the enclosure

- Utilization of 100% recycled cobalt in MagSafe connector magnets - a pioneering feat by Apple
- Integration of 100% recycled rare earth elements in all magnets, representing 99% of such elements in the device
- Adoption of 100% recycled tin in the solder of multiple printed circuit boards
- Application of 100% recycled gold in the plating of multiple printed circuit boards
- Inclusion of 90% recycled steel in the battery tray
- Incorporation of 35% or more recycled plastic in various components

Commitment to Energy Efficiency:

- Endowed with ENERGY STAR® certification

Eco-Friendly Display Innovation

- Display glass crafted without the use of arsenic, ensuring safer materials for both users and the environment.

- Our commitment to sustainability: Eliminating mercury, BFRs, PVC, and beryllium from display components.
- Championing Green Manufacturing: A significant portion (over 30%) of our manufacturing electricity is drawn from clean energy projects initiated by our suppliers, underscoring our dedication to reducing environmental impact.
- Zero waste to landfill: None of our established final assembly supplier sites contribute waste to landfills, a vital step in our eco-conscious manufacturing approach.

Conscientious Packaging Practices

- Responsibly managed forests are the source of 100% of virgin wood fiber used in our packaging materials.
- Aiming for sustainability: More than 99% of our packaging materials are fiber-based, as part of our ongoing efforts to phase out plastic from our packaging.

- Strides toward Our 2030 Environmental Objective: The 15-inch MacBook Air, equipped with the M2 chip, has achieved an impressive 48% reduction in emissions compared to our baseline.
- Apple's Pledge to Environmental Responsibility: Our global corporate operations are already carbon neutral, and our focal point is now on our ambitious Apple 2030 goal to attain carbon neutrality across all our product range.

Acoustic Excellence

- Sound levels adhere to ECMA-109 standards, with declared noise emission values for various operational scenarios.
- Comprehensive Sound Power Level (LWAm) and Sound Pressure Level (LpAm) measurements provide insights into the acoustic performance.
- Wireless web browsing test includes six tabs with varied content, conducted on the M2, 8-

core CPU / 10-core GPU, 8GB unified memory, and 512GB storage configuration.

Note: Be aware that certain technical information and measurements have been condensed or omitted for clarity.

CHAPTER TWO

Setup and Customize your device

Before you can make full use of the features of a brand new Mac computer that you have recently purchased, it is imperative that you setup it with the necessary settings. Even if the process of setting up the device is not unduly complicated, it will take some time if you want to adjust, activate, or deactivate all the settings that are available to you.

Even if you have a MacBook laptop or a Mac desktop, the procedure of setting everything up is exactly the same. In the context of this article, we are going to make the assumption that you are in possession of a brand-new Mac and plan to start the setup process from the very beginning.

Set Location and Accessibility settings

- As soon as you've powered up the Mac Air device, the first thing you'll need to do is select your nation or region.
- You will be prompted with information regarding the setup of particular accessibility features that have been specifically designed to aid with a variety of needs, including vision, hearing, and others.
- Choose which of these qualities you require, if any of them are important to you.
- You also have the option to skip this stage altogether by choosing the "Not Now" button, or you can decide to configure these features at a later point in time.

Connect to Wi-Fi

- In the following step, a connection between your Mac Air device and a wireless network will be established so that the next step may be completed.
- Select the **Wi-Fi network** that you want to use, enter the password for that network, and then click the "Continue" button to move forward.
- Following that is an interface that will provide you an overview of the privacy of your data. Simply clicking "Continue" will take you to the next step, but selecting the "Learn More" link will allow you to investigate this topic in further detail.

Transfer data with Migration Assistant

After that, you will be given the option to utilize the Migration Assistant, which is software that enables the smooth transfer of data from one Mac to another, from a Time Machine backup to a

Windows PC, or from a Windows PC to another Mac.

If you have particular content that you want to move, all you need to do is choose the appropriate option and then proceed through the procedures that follow in order to complete the transfer. If, on the other hand, you choose to postpone taking this action, selecting "Not Now" will not prevent you from making use of the Migration Assistant at a later time, even after the initial setup of your computer has been finished.

Setup Apple ID and Login

In order to proceed, simply follow these steps:

- To begin, head over to the Apple website and enter your Apple ID and password. You can make a whole new Apple ID even if you don't already have one.
- Your Apple ID acts as the portal via which you can access a variety of Apple services. Make

sure that you login in to everything that has to do with Apple using this account.

- In the event that you have already enabled two-factor authentication (2FA) for your Apple ID, a verification code will be sent to your iPhone or iPad. When prompted, enter this code, and then click the **Continue button.**
- After you have finished the two-factor authentication (2FA) process, you will need to click the "Agree" button in order to accept the terms and conditions for using iCloud.

If you follow these instructions, you will be able to successfully create an Apple ID or sign in with an existing one, as well as agree to the terms and conditions of iCloud.

Also, during the process of setting up your device account, simply proceed in the following manner:

- Check that your whole name is listed, and then create an account name that you'll use whenever you login in to your Mac.

- Generate a password and, if desired, offer a hint to help you remember it later.
- Choose the option that will permit your Apple ID to reset this password. This will ensure that your account can be retrieved even if you have forgotten your password.
- Clicking on the image that corresponds to your account name and selecting an image from a list of available alternatives such as memoji, emoji, a monogram, or a photo allows you to personalize your account.
- Simply clicking the "Continue" button will allow you to finish configuring your account.

If you carefully follow these steps, you will be able to correctly configure the settings for your Computer Account.

***Note:* Find My Mac** is an application that, in the event that your Mac is misplaced, can help you find it again with the assistance of the Find My Mac program.

Customize Specific settings

You have arrived at the Welcome Screen for your New Mac's Setup Wizard. You are able to evaluate and make changes to important settings using this screen.

- To proceed, simply click **Continue** if you are happy with the default values for all the settings, or select **Customize Settings** at the bottom of the page to tailor your preferences for location services, analytics, and Siri.
- You have the choice to allow or disable location-based apps like Apple Maps and Weather through the Location Services setting on your device. You can set your time zone by clicking on a location on the map or by selecting the dropdown menu and selecting the city that is closest to you.
- The following step is to consider whether or not you would wish to share analytics with Apple. To have further comprehension of the data collecting and utilization processes,

follow the page labeled "About Analytics and Privacy." Screen Time is a feature that may be activated on this Mac to help manage access to websites and apps. You also have the option to Set It Up Later.

- Mark the checkbox labeled "Enable Siri" on your Mac in order to make use of Apple's speech assistant. If you want to continue using Siri, you will be led through a series of panels that allow you to customize Siri's recognition of your voice.
- If you are satisfied with Apple having access to the audio data on your device, you should enable Share Audio Recordings so that Siri can perform better. You can acquire additional knowledge by selecting the option labeled **About Improve Siri and Dictation & Privacy**. Select **Not Now** to withdraw your consent.
- After that, you will be asked if you would like to encrypt the disk on your Mac using **FileVault**. Increase your system's protection by

selecting the Turn on **FileVault disk encryption option** in the advanced settings. Additionally, check the box next to Allow my iCloud account to unlock my disk in the event that I have forgotten my password.

- You will be walked through the setup process for Macs that come integrated with Touch ID. Tap the Continue button, then take a break from holding your finger on the power button and wait for the registration process to finish. When you are ready to go, click the **Continue button** on your device.
- You can personalize the look of your desktop by choosing between a light mode, a dark option, or Auto, which changes its appearance depending on the time of day. Keep in mind that even after the initial configuration, you can return to the Display settings and make changes to this setting at any time.

Update your Mac

You will get back at your desktop once the installation procedure has been successfully completed. Make certain that your Mac is running the most recent version of macOS as this is the final activity on the to-do list.

- You can upgrade your Mac if it is running macOS Monterey or a previous version by clicking on the Apple symbol, which is located in the top-left corner of your screen.
- Choose "About This Mac" from the menu's submenu, and after that, click on "Software Update." If an update is available, follow the on-screen prompts to choose the "Upgrade Now" option.
- On the other hand, if your Mac is running macOS Ventura or a newer version, you can initiate the upgrade by heading to "System Settings" and then selecting "General" followed by "Software Update." This will take you through the process. If an update is

available, you will be requested to enter your Mac password before the update can begin installing. This happens only if an update is available.

- After the installation of the update has been finished, your Mac will automatically restart, and you will be prompted to sign in again at the login page.

Congratulations! Your Mac is now operating with the most recent version of macOS, which means that you can immediately begin taking advantage of all the new features and enhancements that come packaged with it.

CHAPTER THREE

Basics

Move your files to your new device

Streamline the process of wirelessly moving your files and settings from one Mac or PC to your MacBook Air, whether it's another Mac or another PC. You have the choice to transfer data either from the computer you currently use or from a ***Time Machine backup*** that has been saved to a USB storage device.

It would be helpful if you checked to see if the version of macOS installed on your older computer was compatible with Migration Assistant. It requires macOS 10.7 or later, however upgrading to the most recent version is suggested for maximum performance since it offers the most recent features.

Expert Tip: If you want the best possible results with your new MacBook Air, be sure that it is running the most recent version of macOS. To check for and install any available updates;

- Simply head to the **System Settings menu**
- After that, click on the **General tab**
- And finally, click on the Software Update.

Transfer wirelessly

The Migration Assistant is the tool you should use for wireless file transfers. You are free to use Migration Assistant whenever it is most convenient for you, even if you did not transfer any data during the initial setup of your MacBook Air.

To get started, simply;

- Launch the **Migration Assistant application** by opening a new Finder window, navigating to the Applications folder, clicking to open the Utilities folder, and then double-clicking on its icon.

- Take careful note of the directions displayed on the screen. It is important to bear in mind that both computers will need to be linked to the same network in order for the migration process to be successful, and it is also recommended that they be kept in close proximity to one another.

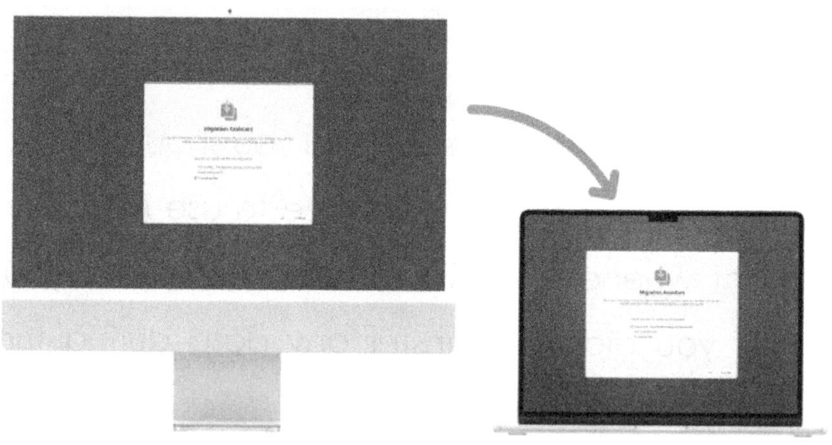

A helpful hint for wirelessly moving data from your current computer to your new MacBook Air is to make sure that both devices are connected to the same network. Keep the two devices within close physical proximity to one another throughout the migration process. This will ensure a smooth transition.

If you have used ***Time Machine*** to create a backup of your data on another Mac onto a storage device, such as an external disk, you have the option to transfer these files to your MacBook Air. This option is available to you in the event that you have used ***Time Machine*** to build a backup of your data.

In order to begin moving data from a storage device to your MacBook Air, you must first connect the device in question to your computer. Let us assume that an adapter is required, check out the list of adapters that are compatible with your MacBook Air. After that, you will need to transfer the data from the external storage device to your MacBook Air by performing an easy drag-and-drop operation.

Backup and restore your new device

A consistent backup of your files on your MacBook Air is required in order to guarantee their safety. Utilizing ***Time Machine***, which is a built-in function of your Mac, is the easiest way to protect your apps, accounts, settings, music, images, videos, and documents (with the exception of your macOS operating system). Use **Time Machine** to create backups on a network volume that is compatible with your MacBook Air or an external storage device that is linked to your MacBook Air.

There are a few steps involved in setting up Time Machine. Verify that your external storage device and your MacBook Air are connected to the same Wi-Fi network, or alternatively, set up a direct connection between the two devices. To access Time Machine, simply;

- Go to **System Preferences**
- After that, select **General** from the menu. You can choose the drive you want backed up by selecting it after clicking the "Add Backup Disk" option.

Keep in mind that data stored in iCloud Drive and photographs stored in iCloud photographs are automatically kept in iCloud and do not require inclusion in your **Time Machine backup**. This is important information for backups that are based on iCloud. However, if you do decide to include them, the following requirements should be followed:

Regarding the iCloud Drive:

- You can access iCloud by going to **System Preferences**, clicking on **your Apple ID**, and then continuing on to iCloud.
- Uncheck the box that says "Optimize Mac Storage" to deselect the option. This will store the contents of your iCloud Drive on your Mac, which will then be included in your backup after it has been completed.

Regarding Apple's iCloud Photos:

- Launch the Photos app, go to the "Photos" tab on the main menu, and then click on "Preferences."

- To enable the "Download Originals to this Mac" option, go to the iCloud tab on your Mac and click the button. Taking these steps will result in the full-resolution versions of all of your photo library's individual images being stored on your Mac, which will then be included in your backup.

Time Machine is a very helpful tool to have in the case that you need to restore some of your files. Simply right-click the Time Machine symbol that is located in the top menu bar and select "Browse Time Machine backups."

Let's say that the **Time Machine symbol** is missing from the menu bar, you can still access it by;

- Going to the Apple menu
- Then, select **System Preferences**
- And after which, select **Control Center** from the sidebar. Find the Time Machine option, and then pick the right course of action to do. You will then be able to proceed with the

"Restore" feature after selecting specific objects to be restored, whether it be individual folders or your full disk's contents.

If your Mac's operating system or startup drive becomes corrupted for any reason, using **Time Machine** to create backups gives you the ability to retrieve lost files. In these kinds of situations, it is absolutely necessary to perform a clean installation of macOS on your Mac before beginning the process of restoring files by using a Time Machine backup.

In the case that macOS is having problems, reinstalling it is an important step to take. The files that make up your operating system are kept safely saved on a disk that is distinct from the disk on which your personal files are kept. On the other hand, a MacBook Air restoration may be required in the event that the disk is deleted or the computer sustains accidental damage. In these kinds of situations, the method entails reinstalling macOS, followed by employing **Time Machine** in order to retrieve your particular data from the backup you had created.

There are a variety of means available for recovering your Mac, beginning with the release of macOS Big Sur and continuing with future versions. It is conceivable that you may need to install a version of macOS that is more recent than the one that was pre-installed on your computer when you purchased it or the version that you were using before the disk became damaged.

Note that there is an option for more experienced users to produce a bootable installer that can be used for subsequent reinstallations of macOS. If you intend to utilize a specific version of macOS that is customized to your liking, this is useful information to have.

Display settings on your Mac device

1. Match the light in your surroundings

Effortlessly come into harmony with your environment. True Tone technology, which is featured on your MacBook Air, is a function that automatically modifies the color of the display so that it is in harmony with the light in the surrounding area. This results in a more genuine visual experience. You can turn on or off True Tone by navigating to the Displays settings inside the **System Preferences menu**.

2. Use a dynamic desktop

Using a Dynamic Desktop can help you achieve a higher aesthetic level. Experience the enchantment of a transforming desktop picture that fluidly adapts to reflect the current time of day in the location you are now in.

You can select a Dynamic Desktop image by going to the Wallpaper section of the **System Preferences**.

Turn on **Location Services** to perform a time zone synchronization depending on your current location. Suppose that **Location Services** are not available, the picture adjusts itself according to the time zone that has been specified in the Date and Time settings.

3. **Stay focused with Dark Mode**

Utilizing **Dark Mode** will help you concentrate better. Choose a sophisticated dark color palette to use for your desktop, menu bar, Dock, and the macOS applications you use the most. Your content is the star of the show, while controls and windows are subtly blended into the background for a more seamless experience. In programs such as Mail, Contacts, Calendar, and Messages, you will be able to read white text on a dark background, which will make it easier on your eyes and reduce eye strain while you are working in low-light settings.

Dark Mode has been rigorously tuned for professionals involved in picture and image processing. Against the backdrop of dark program interfaces, colors and complex details shine out in vivid contrast, making Dark Mode ideal for experts. However, its benefits are available to everyone who wishes to concentrate on their subject without distractions.

4. **Night shift**

Embrace the peace that comes with working the night shift. Change the color scheme on your Mac so that it emits warmer tones at night or in low-light situations. This will help reduce the amount of harsh blue light that reaches your eyes. Warmer screen hues could perhaps lead to a more restful night's sleep by counteracting the effects of blue light, which has been shown to inhibit one's ability to nod off.

You can setup Night Shift to turn on and off automatically at predetermined intervals, or you can set it to be active from the time it becomes dark till the time it gets light. Your choices can be customized by navigating to **System options**, selecting **Displays**, then locating **the Night Shift option** at the bottom of the screen. Adjust the color temperature to your liking by sliding the slider that adjusts it.

5. **Connect a display**

Add another monitor to further enhance the quality of your visual experience. Connecting an external monitor, projector, or HDTV to your Mac is simple and will allow you to increase the amount of space available to you as well as the number of apps you can run.

Window Management on your Mac device

It's easy to feel overwhelmed while trying to manage your digital workplace, which typically manifests as a plethora of open applications and a smattering of windows all over your computer's surface. The management and navigation of windows can be significantly simplified thanks to the existence of appropriate solutions.

In situations where you need to concentrate more intently, you have the choice between making one program fill the entire display or switching to a split-screen mode that allows you to use two apps at the same time. By automating the layout of apps and windows, Stage Manager ensures a clutter-free environment while also facilitating the smooth organization of a desktop and the rapid movement between tasks.

If that you ever face the difficulty of identifying a particular window that has been obfuscated among the others, Mission Control will step in and reveal all the open windows in a cohesive arrangement. In addition, using numerous desktop areas gives you the ability to divide your work across multiple computers, which makes it much easier to switch between different kinds of work.

Engage the Full-Screen View Feature

In order to make use of the entirety of the display that you have, you should activate the full-screen view function. This mode is supported in a smooth manner by a large number of applications on your Mac, including Keynote, Numbers, and Pages.

When you switch to full-screen mode, the navigation bar will gradually disappear until it just touches the top of the display. You also have the option of maintaining permanently visible access to the menu bar.

- Simply move your mouse pointer over the green button located in the top-left corner of the window to enter or exit full-screen mode.
- After that, from the subsequent menu that appears, select "Enter Full Screen."

Harmonize with Split View

Use the Split View functionality to create a harmonic relationship between two app windows so that you don't have to switch back and forth between them. This method functions very similarly to full screen, with the exception that it utilizes two windows that take up the entire screen.

- To begin using this mode, move the pointer to the green button that is located in the top-left corner of the window you have selected.
- After doing so, a menu will appear; from this menu, choose either "Tile Window to Left of Screen" or "Tile Window to Right of Screen."
- When another window is selected, the remaining half of the screen is immediately taken over by that window.
- In addition, while your pointer rests on the green button, a menu cascade will appear. This menu will provide you with options to switch between applications, promote the two windows to full screen, and other options.

Stage Manager

Stage Manager is an easy-to-use application that will help you maintain a clutter-free desktop.

Maintain your primary concentration while keeping all other windows to the side where they may be accessed with a single mouse click.

You can go to ***Stage Manager*** by following these steps;

- First and foremost, open the **Control Center**
- After that, click on the **Stage Manager icon** there.

Mission control

Mission Control will help you to consolidate all of your open windows into a single layer for easier management. Simply clicking on a window returns you to the normal view and makes that window the active one, bringing it to the forefront of the screen.

When you switch to Split View and have more than one desktop (space) or program open, all of them will be displayed in a row at the very top of your screen.

You can enter or leave **Mission Control** by pressing the **Mission Control key**, which is located on the top row of your keyboard, or by utilizing the shortcut Control-Up Arrow. You also have the option of adding an icon for Mission Control to your Dock. Mission Control allows you to control all the open windows and spaces on your computer.

Improve Your Working Environment

If working from a single desktop isn't enough for you, you may increase your productivity by setting up and managing numerous desktops. Simply entering Mission Control and clicking the "Add Desktop" option will allow you to make a new room or area.

Utilize the keyboard shortcuts and Mission Control to seamlessly move between the different spaces. You have the ability to reorganize your workplace however you see fit by dragging windows between the available places.

Learning to Use the Traffic Light Buttons

The trio of red, yellow, and green buttons that are located in the top-left corner of every window serves more than simply cosmetic purposes. There are several functions that are performed by these buttons.

When you click the red button, the app window that you want to close will either be completely closed along with the rest of the program's windows or the current window will be closed while the app continues to operate. When you click the yellow button, the window will be closed momentarily and moved to the right side of the Dock. You may quickly open the window again by clicking its icon in the Dock.

When you click the green button, your windows will quickly switch into full-screen mode, Split View, and other modes.

Keyboard shortcuts

To utilize keyboard shortcuts, follow these steps:

Hold down one or more modifier keys and then press the final key of the shortcut sequence. For instance, to employ the Command-C (copy) shortcut, first press and hold the Command key, then press the C key, and finally release both keys. Mac interfaces and keyboards frequently employ symbols to represent certain keys, including modifier keys:

- Command (or Cmd) ⌘
- Shift ⇧
- Option (or Alt) ⌥
- Control (or Ctrl) ^
- Caps Lock ⇪
- Fn

On keyboards designed for Windows PCs, replace Option with Alt, and Command with Ctrl or the Windows logo key.

Certain keys on specific Apple keyboards possess unique symbols and functions, such as adjusting display or keyboard brightness. If these functions aren't available on your keyboard, you can potentially replicate some of them by creating personalized keyboard shortcuts. To use these keys as standard function keys like F1, F2, F3, combine them with the Fn key.

Common shortcuts for tasks like cut, copy, and paste are as follows:

- To cut the selected item and copy it to the clipboard, use the command-X shortcut.
- Command-C copies the item that is now selected to the clipboard. This shortcut can also be used to copy files in the Finder.
- Command-V will paste the contents of the clipboard into the active document or application; this works for files in Finder as well.
- To undo the most recent command, use Command-Z; to redo it, press Shift-Command-

Z. You have the ability to undo and redo multiple actions within some apps.

- Select all the objects with Command-A.
- Press the Command key and F to search for objects within a document or to open the Find window.
- Find Again can be accessed by pressing the Command key and G. This locates the next instance of the item that was just located. Pressing Shift-Command-G can help you find the occurrence that came before it.
- Press and hold Command-H to hide all windows in the currently active application. By pressing Option-Command-H, you can display only the currently active program while hiding the others.
- To minimize the front window to the Dock, press the Command key and M. Pressing Option-Command-M will minimize all windows of the application that is now active.
- Pressing the Command key and the letter O will either open the currently chosen item or

bring up a dialog box where you may select a file to open.

- To print the current document, press Command + P.
- To save the current document, use Command + S.
- Press and hold Command + T to open a new tab.
- Pressing Command + W will close the active window. To close all program windows at once, use Option-Command-W on your keyboard.
- To force quit an application, press and hold Option-Command-Esc.
- Press and hold the Command key and the Space bar to show or conceal the Spotlight search field. Simply pressing Command, Option, and the space bar will bring up the Spotlight search option within the Finder window. (These shortcuts change the input sources rather than displaying Spotlight if you

utilize several input sources for a variety of languages.)

- To open the Character Viewer, press the Control–Command–Space bar combination. This will make it easier to choose emojis and symbols.
- Pressing Control + Command + F will bring up the full-screen mode for all applications that support it.
- Use the Quick Look function by using the space bar to preview the item you have selected.
- To switch between open applications, press Command-Tab on your keyboard. This will take you to the application that was used most recently.
- Command–Tilde ('): This key combination allows you to switch between windows inside the same application. (The character that appears on the second key varies depending on the keyboard; it is typically positioned to

the left of the number 1 and above the Tab key.)

- Shift-Command-5: If you are using macOS Mojave or a later version, you can take a screenshot or record the screen with this combination. As an alternative, you can take screenshots by pressing Shift-Command-3 or Shift-Command-4.
- Create a new folder in the Finder by pressing Shift-Command-N.
- Command-Comma (,): Opens the settings menu for the currently active application.

Sleep, log out, and short down shortcuts

Note: Be aware that in order to prevent unintended usage of the shortcuts for Sleep, Logging Out, and Shutting Down, you may need to press and hold certain of these shortcuts for a slightly longer period of time than others.

- You can turn on your Mac or bring it back from sleep by pressing the power button. To put your Mac to sleep, press and hold the power button for one and a half seconds. * Keep holding down the power button to force your Mac to shut down.

- Put your Mac to sleep by pressing Option–Command–the Power button* or Option–Command–the Media Eject button.
- Put your displays to sleep by pressing Control + Shift + the Power button or Control + Shift + the Media Eject button.
- If you press Control and then the Power button or Control and then the Eject button, a dialogue box will appear asking you whether you wish to restart, sleep, or shut down the computer.
- Hold down the Control, Command, and Power buttons simultaneously to restart your Mac without being prompted to save any open or unsaved documents.
- Control–Command–Eject Media: Close down all applications, then restart your computer. You will be asked if you wish to save any

unsaved changes to any open documents if any of those documents currently contain unsaved changes.

- Quit all applications before turning off your Mac by using the shortcut Control–Option–Command–Power button or Control–Option–Command–Media Eject. You will be asked if you wish to save any unsaved changes to any open documents if any of those documents currently contain unsaved changes.
- You can immediately lock your screen by pressing Control + Command + Q.
- Using the shortcut Shift-Command-Q, you can log out of your user account on macOS. You will be required to provide confirmation. Pressing Option-Shift-Command-Q will automatically log you out of your account without requiring a confirmation. Note: These keyboard shortcuts are not applicable to the Touch ID sensor.

Shortcuts for the Finder and the System

The following is a list of helpful shortcuts for navigating and carrying out operations within the Finder:

- The command "Command-D" will copy the currently chosen files.
- Ejects the specified volume or disk when you press the Command-E key.
- To begin a Spotlight search in the Finder window, press the Command-F key.
- Use the Command-I shortcut to display the Get Info window for the currently chosen file.
- When an alias is selected in the Finder, show the original file for the alias that has been selected using the command-R shortcut.
- You may need to reload or refresh the page in some applications, such as Calendar or Safari.
- In Software Update, perform another search for available software updates.

- Open the Computer window by pressing Shift-Command-C.
- To open the folder on the desktop, use Shift-Command-D.
- Shift+Command+F will open the Recents window, which will display all of the files that you have recently viewed or modified.
- Shift + Command + G will open a window for going to a specific folder.
- To open the Home folder associated with the active macOS user account, use Shift + Command + H.
- To open iCloud Drive, press Shift-Command-I on your keyboard.
- To open the Network window, press Shift + Command + K.
- Opens the Downloads folder with the Option-Command-L shortcut.
- Create a new folder by pressing Shift-Command-N.
- To open the Documents folder, use Shift + Command + O.

- Show or hide the Preview pane in Finder windows with the shortcut Shift-Command-P.
- Open the AirDrop window by pressing Shift+Command+R.
- Show or conceal the tab bar in Finder windows with the shortcut Shift-Command-T.
- Control-Shift-Command-T (available on OS X Mavericks and later) will add the currently selected Finder item to the Dock.
- Open the Utilities folder by pressing Shift-Command-U.
- Show or hide the Dock by pressing Option-Command-D.
- In versions of OS X later than Mavericks, pressing Control + Command + T will add the currently selected item to the sidebar.
- You can hide or expose the path bar in Finder windows by pressing Option Command P.
- You may hide or expose the Sidebar in Finder windows by pressing Option + Command + S.

- To show or hide the status bar in Finder windows, use Command and the slash character (/).
- Displaying View Options (Command + J).
- Command-K will open the window for connecting to the server.
- Make an alias of the chosen object by pressing Control + Command + A.
- Open a new Finder window with the Command-N shortcut.
- Create a new smart folder with the Option–Command–N shortcut.
- When only one tab is currently open in the active Finder window, pressing Command-T will show or hide the tab bar.
- Option–Command–T: This toggles the visibility of the toolbar in the current Finder window, which only has one tab active at a time.
- Option–Command–V: This command will move the files in the Clipboard from their previous place to the location where they are currently located.

- Command-Y: To preview the files that have been selected, use Quick Look.
- View a slideshow of the selected files in a Quick Look by pressing Option + Command + Y.
- Use the "Command 1" shortcut to display the objects in the Finder window as icons.
- Command 2 allows you to see the contents of a Finder window organized in a list format.
- Command 3 allows you to see the contents of a Finder window organized into columns.
- Command 4 allows you to view a gallery of the objects now displayed in a Finder window.
- Go to the previous folder with the Command–Left Bracket ([) shortcut.
- Go to the next folder with the Command–Right Bracket (]) shortcut.
- Open the folder that contains the current folder by pressing Command and the Up Arrow key.
- Combine the Command key with the Control key and the Up arrow to open in a new

window the folder that includes the current folder.

- Opens the object that was selected with the Command–Down Arrow combination.
- To open the specified folder, press the Right Arrow key. This only works when the list is being seen.
- Left Arrow: Closes the current folder that's been selected. This only works when the list is being seen.
- Using the command and deleting key combination will move the selected item to the trash.
- Delete, followed by Shift, then Command, will empty the trash.
- Delete all items in the Trash without displaying a confirmation dialog by pressing Option–Shift–Command.
- When your Mac is linked to more than one monitor, you can turn video mirroring on or off by using the Command–Brightness Down shortcut.

- Brightness Up is an option that will open the Displays preferences. Both of the Brightness keys can be used with this.
- Control–Brightness Up or Control–Brightness Down: If supported by your display, change the brightness of your external display using these buttons.
- Adjust the brightness of the display in more fine-grained increments by selecting Option–Shift–Brightness Up or Option–Shift–Brightness Down. If your display is capable of supporting external displays, you can perform the change on that display by adding the Control key to this keyboard shortcut.
- Open the Mission Control options by selecting the "Option - Mission Control" menu item.
- Display the desktop, this is Command–Mission Control.
- When you press Control and the down arrow key, the front app will display all of its windows.

- To access the Sound settings, press Option–Volume Up. All the volume keys can be used with this method.
- Adjust the sound volume in incrementally finer steps by selecting Option–Shift–Volume Up or Option–Shift–Volume Down.
- Open the Keyboard settings menu to access the Option–Keyboard Brightness Up setting. The Brightness key on the keyboard can be used for this purpose.
- Adjust the brightness of the keyboard in more fine-grained increments by pressing Option–Shift–Keyboard Brightness Up or Option–Shift–Keyboard Brightness Down.
- When you double-click an item while holding down the Option key, it will open in a new window, and you can then close the window that contained the original item.
- Double-clicking a file or folder while holding down the Command key will open the file or folder in a new tab or window.

- Holding down the Command key while dragging an item to another volume will cause the object to be moved to the other volume rather than copied.
- Pressing the Option key while dragging will copy the item that is being moved. While you are dragging the item, the cursor will change.
- While dragging, holding Option and Command will create an alias of the item being dragged. While you are dragging the item, the cursor will change.
- Click the option button next to the disclosure triangle: Launch each subfolder included within the currently selected folder. This only works when the list is being seen.
- Ctrl-click on the title of the window: View the folders that the current folder is contained within.

You can also access shortcuts for launching several often-used folders by clicking the Go menu in the Finder menu bar. These shortcuts include

Applications, Documents, Downloads, Utilities, and iCloud Drive, among others.

Keyboard shortcuts for formatting text:

- To toggle the bold formatting for the chosen text, press Command-B.
- Toggle the use of italics for the currently selected text with the Command-I shortcut.
- To insert a web link, use Command-K.
- Toggle the use of the underlining formatting for the text that is selected by pressing Command-U.
- You can display or hide the Fonts window by pressing Command-T.
- To select the Desktop folder in the Open or Save dialog box, press the Command-D key.
- Display or hide the definition of the selected word by pressing Control and the letter D.
- Open the Spelling and Grammar window by pressing Shift-Command-Colon (:) on your keyboard.

- Find misspelled terms in the manuscript using the Command-Semicolon (;) shortcut.
- Using the Delete key will get rid of the word that is to the left of the cursor.
- Delete the character to the left of the cursor by pressing the Control key and the letter H.
- To delete the character to the right of the cursor, press the Control-D key on your keyboard.
- On keyboards lacking a dedicated Forward Delete key, using Fn+Delete will perform the same function.
- Using Control-K will delete text from the position of the cursor to the end of the current line or paragraph.
- Scroll up one page with the Fn–Up Arrow's Page Up function.
- Scroll down one page with the Fn–Down Arrow shortcut for the Page Down key.
- Scroll to the beginning of the document when you press the Fn key and the left arrow.

- Scroll to the end of the document using the function key for the right arrow.
- Move the cursor to the beginning of the document by using the Command–Up Arrow combination.
- Use the Command–Down Arrow shortcut to move the cursor to the bottom of the document.
- Moves the pointer to the beginning of the line that you are currently working on.
- Moves the pointer to the rightmost available position at the end of the current line.
- Use the Option–Left Arrow key combination to move the cursor to the beginning of the preceding word.
- Use the Option–Right Arrow key combination to move the cursor to the end of the next word.
- Use the Shift–Command–Up Arrow combination to move the selected text to the beginning of the document.

- Use the Shift–Command–Down Arrow shortcut to select text all the way to the bottom of the document.
- Use the Shift–Command–Left Arrow shortcut to move the current selection of text to the beginning of the line.
- To select text up to the end of the current line, press Shift+Command+Right Arrow.
- Use the Shift-Up Arrow key combination to extend the current text selection to the character above.
- Use the Shift-Down Arrow Key Combination to extend the current text selection to the character below.
- Use the Shift-Left Arrow key combination to move the text selection left by one character.
- Shift and the right arrow key will extend the text selection to the right by one character.
- When you press Option–Shift–Up Arrow, the selection of text will be extended to the beginning of the current paragraph.

- When you press Option–Shift–Down Arrow, the text selection will be extended to the conclusion of the current paragraph.
- Extend the text selection to the beginning of the current word by pressing Option–Shift–Left Arrow.
- When you press Option–Shift–Right Arrow, the text selection will be extended to the end of the current word.
- To move to the beginning of the line or paragraph, use Control-A.
- Move to the end of the line or paragraph by pressing the Control-E key.
- Moves the current character forward by one position.
- Use Control-B to move one character in the reverse direction.
- To center the mouse or selection in the visible area, press the Control-L key.
- Pressing Control + P will move you up one line.
- Move down one line with Control-N on your keyboard.

- To insert a new line behind the cursor, press the Control-O key.
- The Control-T key allows you to move characters around the cursor.

Keyboard shortcuts for Alignment and Formatting:

- Left-align is indicated by pressing Command and the left curly bracket ().
- Right-align is achieved by using the Command–Right Curly Bracket () shortcut.
- The center-align shortcut is Shift–Command–Vertical bar (|).
- Go to the search field by pressing Option + Command + F.
- Show or hide the toolbar by pressing Option-Command-T.
- Copy the current formatting settings to the clipboard by pressing Option + Command + C.
- Option–Command–V: Pastes the copied style into the object that is now chosen.

- Paste while matching the style to the surrounding content by using Option-Shift-Command-V.
- Show or hide the inspector window with the Option-Command-I shortcut.
- Page setup can be accessed by using Shift+Command+P, which will bring up the document settings window.
- Combining Shift and Command with the minus symbol (-) will reduce the size of the selected object.
- Increase the size of the selected object by pressing Shift + Command + the plus sign (+).
- Increase the size of the selected object by pressing Shift + Command + the equal sign (=).
- To open the Help menu, use Shift + Command + the question symbol (?).

Accessibility shortcuts;

- Invert colors by pressing Control + Option + Command + 8.

- Adjust the contrast by pressing Control, Option, Command, and Comma (,) or Control, Option, Command, and Period (.).
- Move the focus to the menu bar with the Control-F2 or Fn-Control-F2 key combination.
- Move the focus to the Dock with the Control-F3 or Fn-Control-F3 keyboard shortcut.
- Move the attention to the active or next window with the Control-F4 or Fn-Control-F4 key combination.
- Moves the attention to the window toolbar and can be activated with either Control-F5 or Fn-Control-F5.
- Move focus to the floating window by pressing Control F6 or Fn Control F6.
- To move the attention to the previous panel, press Control-Shift-F6.
- Toggle the focus behavior of the Tab key with Control-F7 or Fn-Control-F7.
- Move the focus to the status menu with the Control-F8 or Fn-Control-F8 key combination.

- To activate the next open window, press Command and the grave accent (').
- The shortcut for activating the previously active window is Shift–Command–Grave accent (').
- Move the focus to the window drawer by pressing Option–Command–Grave accent (').
- You can navigate between controls by using the Tab key and the Shift-Tab key.
- When a text field is selected, pressing Control and Tab will move you to the next control.
- Move to the previous control grouping by pressing Control-Shift-Tab.
- Use the arrow keys to navigate within menus, tab groups, and list views, as well as to alter value settings.
- Use the control and arrow keys to navigate to the control that is next to the text field.

Always keep in mind that the shortcuts you see here may seem slightly different depending on the app you're working in and the system settings you've chosen to use on your computer.

CHAPTER FOUR

Apple Pay and Touch ID

How to Set Up Apple Pay in Safari on mac

If you want to make a payment using Apple Pay on your Mac, you will need to use Safari, which is Apple's web browser. Safari gives you access to all the different payment choices that Apple Pay offers.

Make sure that your web browser is functional and able to start Apple Pay before you continue with the transactions. The subsequent steps will walk you through the process of configuring Apple Pay on your system running Mac Air device.

Step One:

The first step is to launch the Safari web browser on your Mac's screen.

Step Two:

From the main menu of Safari, select "Preferences."

Step 3:

Once you have opened the preferences window, navigate to the "Privacy" tab and click on it.

Step 4:

On the "Privacy" page, mark the checkbox next to "Apple Pay and Cards" and permit websites to verify Apple Pay and Cards. Click the "Done" button.

After you have completed these stages of configuration, you will be ready to use Apple Pay to make payments quickly and easily whenever it is convenient for you to do so.

How to Set Up Apple Pay on a MacBook with Touch ID

You have the opportunity to approve transactions with Apple Pay by using your keyboard if you have a MacBook Air with the Touch ID fingerprint scanner.

Make sure that your credit card has been connected to your Apple Pay account before you attempt to set up Apple Pay on MacBook Air device. During the first setup of your MacBook Pro or Air with Touch ID, you will normally be requested to provide these information. On the other hand, you can easily add more cards at a later time.

On Macbook Air, here is how to get Apple Pay up and running and manage it:

- Start the **System Preferences application**, which may be accessed from the Applications folder or the Dock on your Mac.

- To open the appropriate window, select "Wallet and Apple Pay" from the menu.
- To enter the details for your debit or credit card, use the "Add Card" option.
- Next, in order to utilize Apple Pay on a MacBook Pro running macOS 11, set it up by following these instructions:

(1) Keep your card within the confines of the frame that appears on your screen so that the FaceTime camera on your Mac may take a picture of it. You also have the option of manually entering the credit card information.

(2) To confirm that your card is valid, click the "Next" button.

(3) Then, enter the three or four digits that appear on the back of your card that are labeled CVC or CVV. In this phase, the validity of the card's expiration date is checked. After you have typed it, click "Next."

(4) By clicking the "Accept" button, you agree to the terms and conditions that have been offered.

(5) Select the form of card verification that you like, either via text message, a phone call, or an email, and then click "Next."

(6) Your chosen verification method will be used to send you a verification code. To continue, enter the code and then click "Next."

Your credit or debit card has been connected to Apple Pay on your Mac successfully, and it is now ready for use. Please be aware that there may be a quick verification process undertaken by your bank, which may result in a little longer wait time than usual. If your application is successful, you will be notified as soon as the verification process is finished.

How to Manage Apple Pay Cards on Your Mac

Using the Touch ID on your Mac, you can quickly and easily configure and manage Apple Pay on your device by navigating to the **System Preferences menu**. You will now have access to transaction data, billing addresses, bank account numbers, and contact information as a result of this, which will allow you to make revisions as necessary and ensure that you retain a complete history of transactions.

To get started, proceed with the following steps:

- Begin configuring your system using the **System Preferences**, which may be accessed from the menu bar or the Applications folder.
- You can open the appropriate window by selecting "Wallet & Apple Pay" from the menu.
- Choose your card from the drop-down menu in the sidebar to gain access to the

transaction details, billing addresses, account numbers, and bank contacts.

How to Change Your Default Apple Pay Card on Mac

When using various cards that are linked to your Apple Pay account on your Mac, you may discover that it is periodically essential to change the card that is selected by default for that account. The amount of available finances as well as any other relevant financial variables may play a role in the outcome of this decision. The settings for the system preferences are where you can make modifications to the card that is set as the default.

The following procedures are advised for users who are working with a Mac that is equipped with Touch ID:

- You can launch the preferences for the operating system by going to the Apple Menu bar or the Applications folder.
- Proceed to the "Wallet and Apple Pay" option by using the menu.
- Choose the credit card that you want to use as the default option from the selection that appears after the initial one.

How to Remove a Card From Apple Pay on Mac

On your Mac device, you can quickly delete a card from Apple Pay in the same way that you can add a card to Apple Pay. You can accomplish this task with the use of Touch ID on your Mac, as well as on your iPhone and Apple Watch.

How to do it:

- Launch System Preferences by selecting "System Preferences" from the Applications folder or the menu bar.

- To access the appropriate window, select Wallet and Apple Pay from the menu.
- Find the card that you wish to get rid of, and then click on it.
- Click the button with the minus sign (-) at the very bottom of the sidebar.
- Click the Delete button to confirm the deletion of the item.

Your card has been successfully withdrawn, and from this point forward, the Apple Pay program that you have installed on your Mac will not allow you to use it to make online payments.

How to Use Touch ID on Mac

Touch ID is a useful supplement to the more conventional technique of logging in with a password, although it might not be able to completely supplant that method.

Despite the presence of this utility, your Mac may on occasion request that you provide a password before it will allow you to proceed. Touch ID, on the other hand, makes the process of signing in to an iOS device much quicker and is useful in a variety of contexts.

You are able to do the following thanks to the Touch ID function on your Mac:

- Unlock your Apple MacBook.
- Make using Apple Pay easier for customers making transactions online.
- Sign into the respective apps and websites.
- Permit purchases made within the app.

It is essential to be aware that not all models of the MacBook come fitted with a Touch ID sensor, which means that you may not be able to use Touch ID on your Mac. Certain versions that have the sensor are the only ones that can take advantage of this functionality.

It is simple to use Touch ID to unlock your Mac, start a purchase in the App Store, or engage in any of the other supported actions. Just put your finger on the Touch ID sensor whenever you're requested to do so. The location of the sensor on the Mac's keyboard is in the upper-right hand corner of the keypad. It goes without saying that you will have to go through the process of setting up Touch ID on your Mac before you can actually utilize it.

How to Set Up Touch ID

When you initially turn on your Mac, your MacBook will remind you to set up Touch ID by displaying a prompt on the screen. You have the option of configuring it right away or delaying the setup until a later time, giving you plenty of options. If you decided to go with the second option and are now ready to set up Touch ID on your Mac, the following steps should be followed:

- Begin by opening the System Preferences window on your Mac.
- Move to the Touch ID section.
- To add your fingerprint, select the option that appears next to the plus sign (+).

- Follow the instructions that appear on the screen: carefully place your finger on the Touch ID sensor, lift it, and then repeat this process many times. Once your fingerprint glows red, this indicates that it is ready, at which point you can click **the Done button.**
- You now have the ability to personalize how the Touch ID feature is used. Check the boxes next to the capabilities that you intend to use Touch ID for, and make sure they are active:

(1) Unlocking your Mac
(2) Apple Pay
(3) iTunes Store
(4) App Store & Apple Books
(5) Password AutoFill
(6) Enable Touch ID on Mac

This brings an end to the process. After completing these easy steps, Touch ID has been successfully set up on your Mac, and you can immediately begin using it.

How to Add, Delete, or Name Fingerprints

Your Mac is capable of storing up to three different fingerprints associated with your user account. After you have Touch ID set up on your iPhone, you will have the option to add additional fingerprints, either your own or those of another person.

- To accomplish this, **go to System Preferences > Touch ID**, and then click the **Add Fingerprint button** once you're there.
- Adding a new fingerprint follows the same steps that the first setup did when it comes to the procedure.
- To give your fingerprint a name, you must first choose it, then click on Finger 1, Finger 2, or whatever its current name is, and then put in the new name. When you are finished entering the new name, press the **Enter key** on your keyboard.
- If you want to remove a fingerprint from your Mac, you may do so by selecting the fingerprint with your mouse pointer and then

clicking **the X icon** that appears. Your Mac will inquire as to whether you are certain about this choice after it has been made. To verify, click the **Delete button.**

Discover the Benefits That Come Along with Employing Touch ID on Your Mac

Accessing your account on your Mac or completing purchases is made a great deal easier thanks to the reliable authentication method that is Touch ID. The tedious process of typing passwords is rendered unnecessary with the introduction of Touch ID. You can gain instant access to your Mac with the tap of a finger, make purchases from the App Store, and take use of a wide variety of additional streamlined features with just a single tap of the screen.

CHAPTER FIVE

Tips to improve Video quality

Video calling has become an extremely popular method for maintaining relationships with loved ones and for taking part in job interviews and other types of meetings while remaining in the comfort of one's own home.

This trend has highlighted the necessity of having high-quality video output, prompting many people to wonder, "How can I enhance video quality on your device?" This chapter elucidates the utilization of the video enhancer, delivering insights into upgrading the video quality to attain top-notch graphics during virtual interactions via platforms such as FaceTime, Skype, Google Hangouts, Zoom, and others.

How to Improve My Video Quality on Calls

There are a number of additional important aspects that, in addition to the technical requirements of the app that you are utilizing, have a considerable impact on the quality of your video conversations.

- **Obtaining the Optimal Distance from the Router**

A sluggish or intermittent internet connection, which is most commonly attributed to weak Wi-Fi connections, is one of the key factors to the quality of a video conversation that is below average. You can resolve this issue by moving closer to the router, which will result in a connection that is both more steady and robust.

In addition, it is of the utmost importance to get rid of any potential impediments, such as walls, that could prevent the Mac from communicating with the router in the most efficient manner possible. Disconnecting other devices, such as those that might be eating up the signal's capacity, resetting the router, or choosing a better frequency band are all ways to obtain further improvements in the signal's strength.

- **Improve the Quality of Your Webcam**

Integration of an external webcam is an alternative method that can improve the quality of video chats made on your Mac. Consider this option. These peripherals are often larger than their built-in counterparts and have the potential to considerably improve the performance of video calls. You have access to a very customizable solution in the form of external webcams because they come with a wide variety of features that can be customized, so affecting both their prices and their capabilities.

- **Making Changes to the Video Quality**

Modifying the settings that control the video quality is one more way to improve the quality of your video call experience when using your device. Acquaint yourself with the options that are accessible inside the operating system to fine-tune the settings of the video quality for increased clarity and performance, and do it as soon as possible.

- **Using Powerline Adapters**

Utilizing powerline adapters is an ingenious solution that may be used to treat homes that suffer from Wi-Fi dead zones, which significantly influence the amount of internet bandwidth available.

You may take advantage of an efficient method that is also beneficial to your wallet by just inserting these adapters into electrical outlets. This will allow you to improve the quality of your internet connection. Because of this, the general standard of the quality of your video calls will immediately and noticeably increase.

Improving the quality of video calls made on your Mac can be accomplished through a variety of methods, including rearranging the physical components, making use of additional hardware, and experimenting with different software configurations. You can ensure that the quality of your video call encounters is always of the highest possible standard by following these guidelines and putting them into action.

How Do I Improve Video Quality on FaceTime

If you feel that adjusting the video quality of FaceTime on your iPhone or iPod is difficult for you, you might want to think about making the switch to a Mac in order to get a better experience overall. This proposal originates from the realization that the video quality can be greatly improved by employing the use of an external webcam.

An unstable internet connection is one of the key difficulties that must be overcome in order to achieve high-quality video calls using FaceTime. It is crucial to ensure that your Mac is linked to a reliable Wi-Fi network in order to offset the effects of this. In addition, in order to achieve the best possible video quality, it is essential for both ends of the call to have robust and reliable internet connections. If you want to get the most out of your bandwidth, you should probably unplug any other devices that are using the same internet connection as you. Place your Mac in close proximity to the router and remove any obstructions that could cause the wireless signal to be disrupted. This will ensure that you receive a strong connection.

Lighting is another important factor that should be considered when trying to improve the quality of your videos captured with FaceTime. The illumination should be directed in front of you, and you should avoid having light sources behind you. Keep motionless and try to avoid moving around too much while the call is in progress. In addition, it is best to avoid standing directly in front of a window or other source of strong light because doing so might provide distracting backlighting as well as excessive motion.

You will be able to dramatically improve the quality of your FaceTime video calls and have conversations that are more interesting and easy to follow if you adhere to these instructions and make the necessary adjustments.

How Can I Improve Video Quality on Skype

At this time, there are no available settings on Skype that are expressly designed to improve the quality of the video stream. However, in order to guarantee the highest possible audio and visual quality during Skype conversations, Microsoft suggests always using the most recent version of the Skype application. Simply clicking on the Skype symbol that is situated in the navigation bar in the top-left hand corner of your display will allow you to validate and update your Skype application.

You are also able to monitor the state of Skype's services through the company's official web page in order to establish whether or not there are any problems affecting the capabilities of the service. Make sure that all of the essential functions, including contact management, instant messaging, media sharing, Skype-to-Skype communication, the payment system, and phone services, are functioning as expected.

If all of these tests show that there are no issues, but you are still seeing low video quality on Skype, you should think about switching internet service providers if the problem persists. It's possible that the problem is related to your present provider's poor signal strength in some instances; if this is the case, switching to a different provider who has a higher bandwidth could potentially fix the issue.

How can I improve Video Quality on Zoom

Recently, many people have found that Zoom is the best option for them when it comes to participating in video conferences. As a result, it is essential to optimize your video settings within the

Zoom program in order to guarantee the experience of the finest possible quality.

The following procedures need to be taken in order to acquire greater image quality and a higher video resolution:

- To get started, navigate to the top right corner of the screen and click on the image of your profile that appears there.
- After that, select the "Settings" option from the menu. Explore the many categories, such as camera, video, and meeting settings, within the menu that is labeled settings.
- In the "Video" section of the menu, you will see a choice labeled "Enable HD." You can make a considerable improvement to the overall video quality by selecting this menu option.
- In addition, it is of the utmost importance to verify that your camera satisfies the specified requirements, as this has a direct impact on the resolution as well as the quality of the video.

In addition, if you want to watch videos without interruptions, you should work to improve the quality of your internet connection. In order to accomplish this, you should think about disconnecting any other devices that might be using the same internet connection so that you can free up some bandwidth. Put yourself in close proximity to the router so that you may establish a connection that is both stronger and more reliable.

By adhering to these recommendations, you can make certain that the visuals of your Zoom video conferences are of the highest possible quality and that the experience as a whole is improved.

CHAPTER SIX

Text Messages

Apple's Messages app has a fantastic feature that allows you to synchronize all of your text messages across all of your devices, including iPads, iPhones, and Macs. However, in order for this synchronization to work, it is necessary for each device to maintain a consistent log-in to the same Apple ID. It is really impressive that Apple takes care of iPhone users who do not use iMessage by assuring compatibility with SMS text messages as well as those who utilize iMessage.

How to Get Text Messages on Your Mac

You will need to properly configure the Messages app on your Mac air device before you will be able to begin receiving text messages. To be of assistance to you, the following is a step-by-step guide:

- Start using Messages by opening the Messages application from your Applications folder, Dock, or Desktop.
- Sign in using your Apple ID: If this is the first time you've launched Messages on your Mac, you will be prompted to enter the email address and password associated with your Apple ID. Also, submit the verification code if you have two-factor or two-step authentication turned on in your account.
- Adjusting Your Access Settings: In the top menu bar, pick "Messages," then choose "Preferences" from the drop-down menu that appears.
- Installing iMessage requires going into the Preferences window, selecting the "Accounts" tab, and then selecting "iMessage."
- Configure Your Contact Information: Once you have successfully logged in, you will have

the opportunity to enter the telephone number and email address at which you would like to receive communications. You can customize the default phone number and email address that will be shown whenever you start a new chat by clicking the corresponding buttons. Simply clicking on the option and picking a different one will change the default setting.

- Enable Forwarding of Text Messages: Taking the following steps will ensure that you are able to receive text messages on your Mac in a timely manner:

a) On your iPhone, sign in with the same Apple ID that you use on your computer.

b) Navigate to "Settings" on your iPhone, and then pick "Messages."

c) Scroll to the bottom of the page and select "Text Message Forwarding."

d) To enable or stop text message forwarding on your Mac, toggle the switch that is located on the keyboard.

- Maintain Connection on iPhone: Before doing anything else, check to see that your iPhone is powered on and connected to the internet. This will ensure that any new text messages you get are routed to your Mac as soon as they are received.
- You are now able to send and receive iMessages and text messages using the Messages app on your Mac device. Once you have finished the setup and turned on Text Message Forwarding, you can do so now.

Keep in mind that if you continue to use Messages on your Mac air device, you will have the ability to easily respond to incoming text messages right from your computer.

If you follow these instructions, you will be able to integrate text messages between your iPhone and Mac, which will make it much easier for you to handle your texts across all of your devices.

How to Get Messages in iCloud in mac

The following actions need to be taken in order to synchronize messages between macOS 11 and iCloud:

- Make sure that your Apple ID is properly logged in your device.
- Go to the **Settings menu** on your iPhone.
- Select your Apple ID account at the very top of the screen.
- Choose iCloud, then activate Messages by turning the switch to the "On" position.
- Launch the Messages application located on your Mac.
- To access your messages, select "Messages" from the menu bar.
- Also, select the **Preferences menu option.**
- Proceed to the tab labeled "iMessage."
- To synchronize your iCloud data and messages with your Mac, you need to ensure that the box labeled "Enable Messages in iCloud" is checked.

If you are having problems with messages not showing, you might want to explore the following solutions:

- Make sure that you are logging into both your Mac and your iPhone with the same Apple ID. Syncing might become problematic when many accounts are used.
- Make sure that your iPhone is connected to a reliable cellular or Wi-Fi network. If there are problems with connectivity, try turning Wi-Fi off and then back on again.
- If you continue to have issues with your Wi-Fi connection, you could try to reconnect to the network. Simply disconnect from the Wi-Fi network, then re-establish the connection while entering the password again.
- Let's asssume that network-related remedies are unsuccessful, you should reset your network settings. This step will not have any impact on the apps or data on your device;

however, you will need to reenter your Wi-Fi passwords.

- You should temporarily deactivate the forwarding of text messages on your iPhone, then reactivate it later while making sure the same Apple ID is utilized.
- It is recommended that you delete superfluous messages from Messages in iCloud in order to make more storage space and maybe improve synchronization. Navigate to the Messages app on your iPhone by going to **Settings > General > iPhone Storage > Messages**. Tap the **Edit button** to choose the files, then select and delete the media.

You can enable message synchronization on mac air device by following these steps, and you can also resolve problems that may occur, such as messages not showing even though they were sent.

CHAPTER SEVEN

Steps to screenshot on Mac Air Device

There is a key on the keyboard of a Windows computer that is referred to as the **Print Screen key**, and users press this key to take screenshots. On the other hand, there is no analogous special key for taking screenshots on Apple computers, such as Mac air device.

Users have the option of using shortcuts on their keyboards or built-in applications, such as Preview, which is a component of Mac operating systems. These techniques offer a number of benefits, the most significant of which are their ease of application and their briskness. Are you curious about how to capture the screen of your MacBook? Investigate the information that is presented in this chapter in order to get the necessary knowledge.

How to Take a Screenshot with Keyboard

Taking screenshots on your Mac air device by using the keyboard shortcuts included into the Mac operating system is a simple and efficient process. Whether you need to capture the entire screen, a specific portion of it, or just one window, these commands make it easy to accomplish any of those three tasks. The following will provide you with in-depth descriptions of each strategy.

a. Capture the Entire Screen:

On your Mac air device, there are two different ways that you can easily capture the display of your entire MacBook:

- The first method requires you to simultaneously press Command + Shift + 3 on your MacBook in order to take an instant screenshot.

- The second method is to copy the image to your clipboard, press and hold the Command key while also pressing and holding the Shift key, followed by the Control key.

b. Capture a Particular Region

You have a few alternatives when it comes to taking a picture of a particular region, which are as follows:

- Method 1: To turn your pointer into a crosshair, hold down the Command key and simultaneously press Shift and 4 on your keyboard. Simply construct a selection by clicking and dragging the mouse around the area of interest. As soon as you let go of the button on the mouse, the screenshot will be saved to your desktop.
- Method 2: If you would rather save the information to the clipboard instead, you can do it by simultaneously pressing the

Command, Shift, 4, and Control keys. The arrow on the cursor changes into a crosshair; click and drag the mouse to outline the capture area.

c. Taking a Screenshot of a Single Window

In order to take a screenshot of a single window, follow these steps:

- Simply by hitting Command, Shift, and 4 all at the same time, you may turn your pointer into a crosshair. To save the contents of the clipboard, press the keys Command + Shift + 4 + Control.
- When you press the space bar, the cursor transforms into a camera symbol, and the screen takes on a bluish-gray hue.
- When you move your mouse over the window you want, a light blue highlight will appear over it. You will need to select the window that

you want to capture before the image can be saved to your desktop.

It is essential to keep in mind that this method does not just record windows but also the desktop, the menu bar, the Dock, and any open menus.

In addition, the image that was saved included not just the window but also its shadow superimposed over a see-through background. You have the option to save the image without the shadow if you choose by holding down the **Option key** as you click to do so.

How to Take a Screenshot without Keyboard

You may be wondering, "Is there an alternative method for taking screenshots on your Mac device without relying on keyboard commands?" You are able to make use of the Preview program, hence the answer is yes to this question.

Since it eliminates the need to memorize certain key combinations, the Preview app is especially helpful for people who only sometimes take screenshots. This is because it removes the need to memorize specific key combinations.

The following steps need to be taken in order to use Preview on Mac air device in order to capture the screen of your MacBook:

- Find the folder labeled "Applications," and then open it. You can start the Preview app from that location.
- You can take a screenshot by going to the "Files" menu and selecting "Take Screen Shot." There are a few different capture options accessible inside this menu, including the current window, the entire screen, or a particular section of the screen.
- If you select "From Entire Screen," a helpful countdown of ten seconds will begin. This gives you plenty of time to get the screen

ready for capturing according to your preferences before the timer goes out.

When you take a screenshot on your device and simultaneously click **the Control key** on your keyboard, Preview will automatically transfer the image to your clipboard. It is important to note that these captures, in contrast to those made using keyboard instructions, are not instantly stored to your desktop.

The Preview feature gives you the option to manually save the photographs, giving you the freedom to give them any name and save them in any location of your choosing. You also have the option of removing any screenshots from consideration that do not fulfill your criteria. In addition, because the screenshots open within the Preview app, you have the ability to make any necessary modifications to them in the event that they are required.

CHAPTER EIGHT

Record FaceTime calls

Due to its user-friendly design, cost-effectiveness, and exceptional high-definition video capabilities, the FaceTime application stands out as a highly popular alternative for making group video conversations. This popularity can be ascribed to the app's impressive qualities. FaceTime develops as a vital tool for sustaining connections with loved ones in an era that is characterized by the requirement of maintaining social distance and diminishing physical mobility.

There may be times when you feel it is absolutely necessary to record and save a FaceTime call on your Mac air device, whether it be for future reference or for your own personal use. Within the scope of this tutorial, we will offer you with in-depth instructions on how to successfully record a FaceTime call using your Mac air device.

How can I Record FaceTime Call on My mac

Video and photos are excellent ways to preserve cherished memories and maintain records of important events or objects. FaceTime, a program available on your device, enables you to make group calls with family, friends, or colleagues in your professional network.

Family moments are often filled with joy, and occasionally, you may wish to record a FaceTime call on your device to capture these precious memories.

Let's explore the significance and advantages of FaceTime calls:

- **Staying Connected:** FaceTime calls help you stay in touch with family and friends, regardless of their location within the same country or overseas.
- **Business Collaboration**: For business purposes, FaceTime calls facilitate seamless communication among teammates within the same company. This makes it easier to discuss and coordinate on specific projects or operations.

- **Cost-Effective Communication**: Using FaceTime calls can be more economical than subscribing to expensive calling plans when communicating with individuals located in other countries.
- **Versatility:** FaceTime allows you to switch between video and audio calls, providing flexibility to communicate based on your preferences and needs.

To record a FaceTime call on your Mac Air device, you can use the built-in Screen Recording tool. However, if you are using an earlier mac version like Mojave or Catalina, QuickTime can be utilized for the same purpose.

How to Record FaceTime Calls

Follow these easy steps on your Mac Air device in order to record a FaceTime call:

- **Step 1:** Navigate to the Applications folder on your Mac and then launch the QuickTime application there.

- **Step 2:** At the very top of the screen, click on the "File" option, and then select "New Screen Recording."
- **Step 3:** In the control bar for the screen recording that has now shown, click the arrow that is located next to the "Record" button. Make "Internal Microphone" the source of your audio by selecting it. Now, launch the FaceTime program by navigating to the Applications folder and selecting it from there.
- **Step 4**: While FaceTime is still open, navigate to the QuickTime window and click the "Record" button. You can customize the area that will be recorded by dragging the boundaries until they completely enclose the FaceTime window. Alternately, you can record the entire display simply by clicking anywhere on the screen.
- **Step 5:** Once you have started your FaceTime call, QuickTime will begin to record both the screen and the audio. To end recording the FaceTime call, when the call is over, click the

"Stop Recording" option in QuickTime. This will save the recording.

- **Step 6**: Navigate back to the "File" menu, and this time, choose "Save." You will be prompted to give a name for your recorded FaceTime session and select a destination. Click the "Save" button at the bottom of the screen to finally save the recording.

Following these instructions will allow you to easily record your FaceTime calls while using the Mac Air version of the QuickTime program.

CHAPTER NINE

Download Apps on your device

Applications are an essential component in expanding the capabilities of our gadgets and endowing them with a unique personality, and this role is becoming increasingly important. They are essential to the smooth running of operations, the improvement of communication, the execution of commercial activities, and the efficient administration of commodities. Incorporating all the necessary software into your device is quite necessary if you want to achieve the most possible performance from it.

The Mac App Store acts as a central location that has a wide variety of programs and applications that are specifically designed to meet your requirements when you are looking to improve your experience with your device. You may, however, run into a problem when attempting to download applications from the Mac App Store. This may become a barrier for you. In such a situation, what are some ways that you can get over this barrier and effectively buy software from the Mac App Store so that you can take full advantage of the benefits they offer?

Why Should we Download Apps from the Mac App Store

The Mac App Store makes a wide variety of software programs readily available for download, and it can all be done in the convenience of one's own home or office. Although it is feasible to acquire apps from third-party sources, it is essential to be aware of the potential negatives that may be associated with doing so. The Mac App Store provides a larger selection of applications that are compatible with your device than the majority of third-party platforms provide. When compared to other download providers, this means that there is a greater probability of finding the precise application that you require.

In addition, making the decision to only download applications from the Mac App Store provides a considerable benefit in terms of the reliability and safety of the software you use. Every application that is listed in the Mac App Store is put through stringent testing at multiple stages to guarantee that it is safe to use and does not include any viruses or other forms of dangerous malware. On the other hand, third-party sources do not have this level of protection, which means that users may be exposed to corrupted or malicious files that could put their devices at risk.

You have the benefit of being able to read reviews written by other customers and obtain additional information about each application before you decide to download any of them from the Mac App Store. You will find that the majority of the offers in the Mac App Store give detailed explanations of the tools and features. This will assist you in assessing whether or not a specific app meets your requirements. In addition, user evaluations provide insights into the legitimacy of the app because they originate from users who have firsthand experience with the program being reviewed.

When compared to other third-party platforms or websites, the Mac App Store has a number of advantages that users can take advantage of when they make the decision to download applications from there solely. On the other hand, it is important to be aware that some users can have trouble downloading applications from the Mac App Store when using your Mac Air device.

Download App from the Mac App Store

Are you having trouble downloading apps from the Mac App Store while using your Mac Air device? There Is No Need to Be Afraid! Using the steps in this guide, you will be able to successfully download the application of your choice from the Mac App Store.

- Step 1: The first thing you need to do is open the Mac App Store application. You may do this from the Dock, Launchpad, or by using Spotlight search. When the app store is opened, look for the app you want to download and click on its icon.
- Step 2: Navigate to various application categories by clicking on the tabs that are located on the left-hand side of the window that displays the Mac App Store. In this section, you also have the option to look through the featured apps.
- Step 3: Depending on the status of the app, either the "Get" or "Price" button will be active for you to click. To begin the download of an app at no cost, pick "Get" and follow the on-screen instructions. To purchase and download a paid software or tool from the Mac software Store, select "Price" from the

menu bar and then follow the on-screen instructions.

- Step 4: When you click "Get," a notification about the installation will be triggered, and the button will turn green. If you choose to use a paid app, tapping the "Price" button will cause it to become green and will bring up a popup asking you to "Buy App."
- Step 5: In order to begin the download, you will need to check in with your Apple ID, input your password, and then enter your Apple ID.
- Step 6: The download of the chosen application will now begin. When the download is finished, the application can be found in the Application folder that is part of Finder on your computer. There is also a possibility that it will show up on the Launchpad of your Mac Air operating system.

You can also consult Apple's official resources or support channels for further assistance or troubleshooting information. Apple makes both of these available.

CHAPTER TEN

Dark Mode

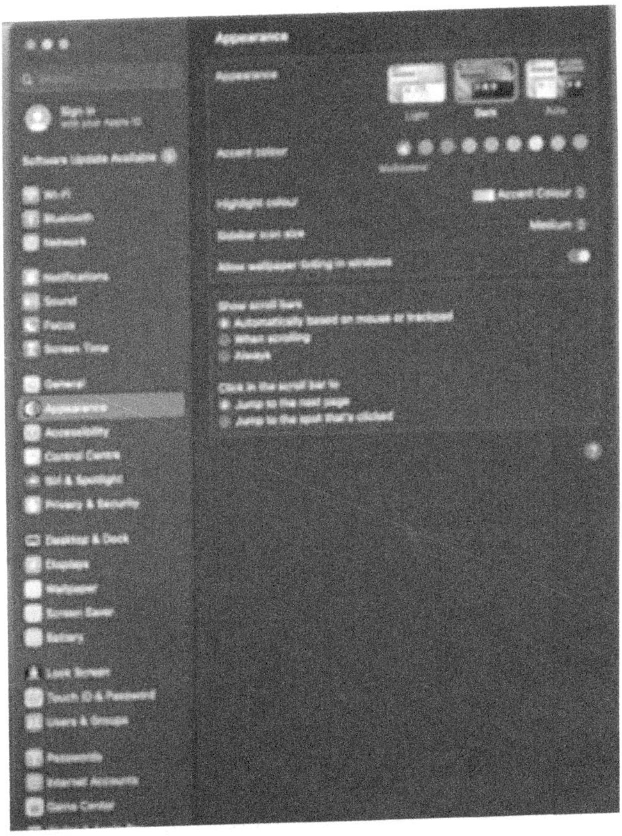

According to the vast majority of people who use Macs, switching to Dark Mode is helpful for improving focus throughout a variety of Mac activities, including work. This is because Dark Mode is able to highlight information while simultaneously lowering the prominence of darkened buttons and windows in the background.

One of the most significant benefits of utilizing Dark Mode is that it employs a dark color scheme all throughout the operating system, making it easier on the eyes. This indicates that not only are you able to take advantage of its benefits while utilizing native apps like Safari, but you are also able to effortlessly extend its benefits to third-party applications.

What is Dark Mode?

Dark Mode is a compelling new feature that was introduced in Mac Air device. This feature gives customers the ability to alter the way their theme looks once they have updated their Mac. If you're used to working in the Light mode, this specific device presents an ideal opportunity to experiment with a new aesthetic by switching to the Dark mode.

This aesthetic option is intended to improve content visibility by forcing controls and windows to fade into the background, so providing a better overall focus. It does this by drawing attention away from the foreground elements (such as the content itself).

However, it is crucial to keep in mind that certain programs and functions will have their distinct aesthetic preferences and may overrule the settings that are determined by Dark Mode. This is because Dark Mode alters the appearance of the operating system on a system-wide scale, which affects many components of the operating system.

Finder, Safari, Photos, Notes, Apps, Mail, and Music are just some of the built-in applications that take advantage of the aesthetics offered by Dark Mode. In addition, you will be glad to learn that a large number of third-party applications are also prepared to support this functionality. This will provide you with a unified and immersive user experience across your entire Mac system.

How to Turn on Dark Mode

To activate Dark Mode on your system, perform the following steps:

1. **Step 1: Access the System Preferences**

You can access the System Preferences menu in a number of different ways. You can use Spotlight by typing "system preferences," find it in the menu bar by clicking on the **Apple icon,** or open it from Launchpad by pinching four fingers together. All of these options are accessible through the Apple icon.

2. **Step 2: Locate general**

After **System Preferences** has been launched, direct your attention to the top row of icons, which is often found on the left side of the window. Choose "General" from these available selections;

the "General" area of the preferences panel on your Mac contains the settings that control its colors and its overall design.

Step 3: Select the Appearance menu option

The "Appearance" heading can be found at the very top of the window that is devoted to changing one's appearance. You'll see that the following options have been distinctly indicated below this:

- "Light" for the purpose of activating the Light mode
- "Dark" to activate the Dark mode in the game.
- "Auto" to perform an automatic transition between the Light mode during the day and the Dark mode during the night.

To access Dark Mode, choose the "Dark" option from the drop-down menu. If, on the other hand, you want to utilize Dark Mode on your Mac air device only when it is nighttime, you should select the **Auto option** instead.

How to Use Dark Mode in Pages

You have the ability to create wonderful papers with the help of Pages for Mac, which is a powerful word processor that comes preinstalled on your laptop. It provides you with the instruments you need to customize fonts and include eye-catching visuals into your work.

On the other hand, if you activate Dark Mode in your device, Pages might not adjust to the new display setting. The documents that you generate within this program are formatted in a way that makes them suitable for printing by default. This means that you will continue to compose your documents using black text on a white canvas.

You have the opportunity to change the layout to suit your needs, and one of those options is a darker workspace for you to type in. Changing the color of the backdrop and storing the altered template for later usage are both required steps in this process.

Follow these methods to get a background that looks good in Dark Mode when you use Pages:

- Open up **Pages,** and then open a brand new, empty document.
- Place a shape, such as a square, in the upper-left hand corner of the canvas.
- You can adjust the size of the shape by dragging the corner on the bottom right of it until it fills the full page.
- Check to see that the shape completely fills the page.
- Make the shape's color black using the color picker.
- To make this the background for all pages, go to Arrange > Section Master, and then move the item you want to use to the Section Masters layer. This will make it the background for all pages.
- Use the Update function to make the text white instead of the default color of black.

If you follow these instructions, you will be able to create a background for Pages that is compatible with the device Dark Mode. Because of this, the setting will be more visually comfortable for you, particularly when you utilize it in the evening.

How to Use Dark Mode in Safari

In its capacity as an integrated web browser, Safari for Mac provides users with a streamlined experience across a variety of websites for conducting online research and reading articles.

When you turn on Dark Mode on your Mac, Safari immediately begins rendering websites with a Dark Mode theme, giving priority to those websites that have been specifically optimized to take advantage of this aesthetic. Safari provides an efficient solution in the form of its Safari Reader function for situations in which a website does not provide support for the Dark Mode setting.

The objective of Safari Reader is to offer webpage articles in a clean layout that is devoid of distractions and is optimized for increased readability by removing features such as adverts.

In order to get this process started:

- On your Mac, you can access the Safari application by going to the Applications folder.
- In the event that a website hosts an article that is compatible with Safari Reader, the Reader View symbol will appear in the upper left-hand corner of the Safari address bar.
- On your device, the icon that looks like the letter "aA" can be found in the upper right-hand corner of the Safari address bar. Clicking this icon will enable Dark Mode for your reading experience. By selecting this alternative, you will be able to switch to the backdrop color that is the darkest while still maintaining the ability to modify the font size and style. It is essential that you take into account the fact that Safari will save these adjustments for later usage.

- To exit Safari Reader and return to the standard mode of viewing, please do one of the following:

a. To exit **Reader View**, either re-click the icon on the toolbar or press the "Esc" key on your keyboard.

If you follow these steps, you will be able to enhance your browsing experience on Safari for Mac in a way that is seamless, especially when using the Dark Mode in your Mac Air device.

CHAPTER ELEVEN

Tips to save Battery

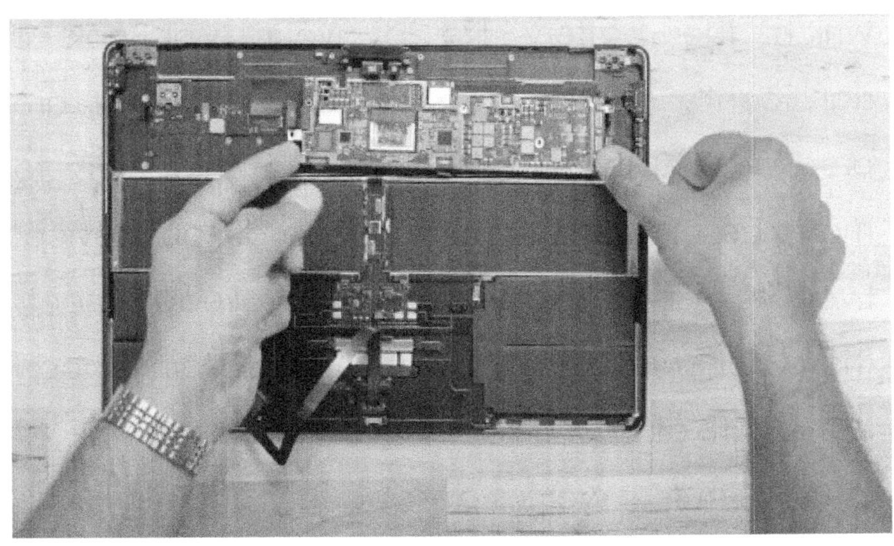

The longer battery life of Apple's MacBook computers is partly attributable to the improved efficiency of its CPUs, and this improvement is made possible by the release of new models of the MacBook every year. Take, for example, the MacBook Air 2018/2019, which claims an outstanding battery life of up to 13 hours when streaming media via the Apple TV app and up to 12 hours when wirelessly browsing the internet. This constitutes a significant change from what came before it.

On the other hand, if you run into a situation in which the battery life of your MacBook is significantly shorter than the durations that are predicted, it is vital that you take actions to maximize the battery performance of your device. Even if your MacBook Air device already meets these benchmarks, it is still vital to maintain a good battery life on your device in order to assure a bright future with few worries over battery depletion. This will allow you to make the most of your device's potential.

In essence, when fresh models of the MacBook are released every year, their battery efficiency continues to increase. This is shown by the extraordinary durability of the MacBook Air 2018/2019. Maintaining or even improving the battery life of your MacBook in the environment of your device requires attention and care to provide a smooth and long-lasting user experience. However, this can be accomplished with the proper attention and care.

How to improve battery life on your MacBook

1. **Adjust the Brightness of the Display**

Dimming the display on your Mac computer is one of the simplest ways to extend the life of the battery. Dimming the display helps the battery last longer because it uses less energy than having it at its maximum brightness setting. Find a level of brightness that is tolerable for your eyes while maintaining an appropriate amount of energy efficiency.

To accomplish this,

- Go into **System Preferences**
- Afterwards, select **Energy Saver** from the menu, and then configure the display such

that it dims somewhat while it is not being used.

- In addition, if you are in a bright setting, you should turn off the auto-brightness feature by going to System Preferences > Display and unchecking the box that says "Automatically adjust brightness."

2. Maintain Current Software Versions

Using software that is up to date on your device will help you get longer battery life out of your MacBook Air device. Checking for available updates should be done on a regular basis by;

- Navigating to **System Preferences > Software Updat**e.
- Streamline the process of updating by selecting "Automatically keep my Mac up to date" and specifying advanced parameters to automatically download and install updates.

This will make it so that your Mac is always up to date.

3. **Take Control of the Keyboard's Backlights**

Protect the life of the battery by limiting the use of the keyboard backlight. If you use a keyboard with backlighting, you should program it to switch off after a certain amount of time of inactivity.

You can tailor the "Turn keyboard backlight off after" option in the System Preferences > Keyboard menu to your specific needs by adjusting the amount of time that passes between typing sessions.

4. **Turn off Bluetooth while it's not being used**

When not in use, Bluetooth should be turned off to preserve the life of the battery.

- To disable Bluetooth, either click the **symbol** that appears in the menu bar;
- Or navigate to the **System Preferences menu** and select **Bluetooth.** It is more efficient to

save battery by turning Bluetooth off, especially if you aren't utilizing any Bluetooth devices, such as speakers or mice.

5. **Close any unused applications**

On your Mac Air device, quitting applications that aren't being utilized helps preserve the life of your MacBook Pro's battery. You can quit the application by using the keyboard shortcut **Command + Q,** or you can select the "Quit" option from the menu that appears in the menu bar. Determine which programs/apps are consuming your power supply by monitoring your energy consumption in the Activity Monitor's Energy tab.

6. **Make use of the Dark Mode.**

On your Mac Air device, switching to Dark Mode can help save battery life, as pixels with a black color require less energy to function than those with a white color.

To activate Dark Mode, simply;

- Head over to **System Preferences > General**
- Afterwards, select "Dark" from the drop-down menu.
- Alternately, you can change the colors by going to System Preferences > Display and checking the box that says "Invert Colours."

7. Control the Activities Going On in the Background

Managing the operations that run in the background might lengthen the battery's life. To cut down on the amount of power consumed:

- **Reduce the number of notifications:** Simply head over to Notifications > System Preferences to reduce the number of times apps check for notifications.
- **Turn off spotlight**: Spotlight may be turned off by going to System Preferences > Spotlight >

Privacy >. Include the hard disk on your Mac in the list that is reserved for privacy.

- **Modify the mail's automatic check**: Simply head over to General > Mail > Preferences > Adjust your settings so that "Check for new messages" is set to "Manually."

8. Keep the Temperature at an Optimal Level.

Avoid letting your MacBook's battery become too hot by preventing overheating. Placing your MacBook on a stand will allow air to flow underneath it, which will prevent it from being overheated. Keeping the temperature of the operating environment at a low level helps extend the life of batteries.

9. Avoid Overcharging

Avoid overcharging the battery in order to avoid damaging it. After your MacBook has finished charging, disconnect it from its power source and consider only charging it to around half capacity before storing it. When the battery percentage is at a very low level, you should try to limit the amount of use you give your MacBook.

10. Turn Off Any Features That Are Drawing Too Much Power

Disabling functions that use a lot of power will allow you to get even more use out of your battery.

- When you're not using Wi-Fi, make sure it's turned off.
- Disconnect any hardware that isn't necessary: When not in use, SD cards, modems, and external devices all drain power and should be removed from the device.

If you follow these instructions, you will be able to efficiently maximize the battery life of your MacBook Air device and ensure that it will last as long as possible.

The Internet

Wi-Fi, Personal Hotspot, and Ethernet: How to Get the Most Out of Your Internet Connections

1. **Getting Connected to a Wi-Fi Network**

- Simply select the **Wi-Fi option** from the menu bar on your device in order to connect to a wireless network.
- Once you're there, choose the network you want to use.
- Before you may connect to the network, you might be required to provide the network password or give your approval to the terms and conditions first.

2. **Leveraging the Potential of Your Own Personal Hotspot**

It is possible to share the cellular data connection that your iPhone or iPad uses (Wi-Fi + Cellular) with your Mac for users who have carrier plans that are compatible with this feature. Get yourself acquainted with the procedure of configuring and employing Personal Hotspot for the purpose of this activity.

3. **Taking Advantage of Connectivity Provided by Ethernet**

You can also create a reliable wired internet connection by creating a physical link using an Ethernet cable that is plugged into the Ethernet port on your Mac and into the Ethernet port on your router or modem.

There are some Mac models that may require an Ethernet adapter, such as the Apple Thunderbolt to Gigabit Ethernet Adapter or the Belkin USB-C to Gigabit Ethernet Adapter. Both of these adapters are available through Belkin.

How to Use Safari

As the primary web browser application, Safari is pre-installed on all Macs and comes standard as part of macOS. Despite this, you are not required to use Safari in every single instance. If you want to use a different web browser, such as Chrome or Firefox, you may easily install that software and use it for all of your web browsing needs.

Having said that, Safari stands out as an appealing option based on our previous experiences with it. The fact that we chose Safari as one of the best web browser applications for the Mac demonstrates that it is without a doubt one of the best choices accessible.

This primary focus is on assisting readers who are new to the Safari web browser in becoming familiar with the application's interface. Even if you think of yourself as an experienced Safari user, you should still read this article since it contains a few tips and tricks that aren't as widely known, including information about Safari 11, which is the most recent version of Safari for Mac.

Getting Familiar with the Safari Web

Browser

If you're just getting started with Safari, the following suggestions can help you become more familiar with the program:

Let's start with the basics, such as how to launch Safari, do searches, and other helpful hints and tips. If you already have a firm grasp on these fundamentals, feel free to jump forward to the next section. In the following paragraphs, you will discover a plethora of helpful hints that are sure to be of interest to you.

The Dock, which is positioned at the bottom of the screen on your Mac, provides access to the Safari web browser. It has an icon that looks like a compass.

Making use of Safari

Your connection to the rest of the internet is made through the conspicuous bar at the top of the Safari window. You have the option of entering a search keyword or the URL of a website. You can use this to either directly navigate to a certain website or see a list of pages that match your search parameters. Both options are available to you.

You have the ability to change the default search engine that Safari uses, which is configured to be Google by default. If you prefer to use a different search engine, you have that option.

In most circumstances, it is not required to input the full URL. When you have previously been to a website, simply inputting a few letters of its name will cause an autofill function to activate, which will then finish typing the URL for you.

For example, if you write 'Face,' Safari will automatically finish completing the URL for you, and after you hit Enter, you will be taken directly to Facebook.

How to Manage Tabs

By utilizing tabs rather than individual windows, as is the case in a lot of apps, you have the ability to reduce the total number of windows that are active on your computer's desktop.

For example, you can use **TextEdit** to create a single window that contains a tab bar that contains several tabs. This tab bar is located beneath the formatting options. The **Close button** in the window is displayed on one of these tabs, and an **Add button** can be found at the rightmost end of the tab bar.

The following actions need to be taken in order to determine when documents should open in tabs:

- To access the system preferences on your Mac, go to the **Apple menu** and then choose "System Preferences."
- Next, on the sidebar, select "Desktop & Dock" and click it. It's possible that you'll need to scroll down to find it.

- You'll discover a dropdown menu to the right of the "Windows & Apps" area that's labeled "Prefer tabs when opening documents." Select the item that best suits your needs from the options.
- Even if the "Prefer tabs when opening documents" setting is configured to "Always," you can rapidly launch a new window within an application by pressing the Option-Command-N shortcut key combination. This is a pro tip.

The following actions need to be taken on your Mac in order to add tabs to a document:

- Start by opening a file, for example in the app called **TextEdit.**
- Either click the "New Tab" button that is located in the tab bar or navigate to the "File" menu and select the "New Tab" option (if it is available).

- If the tab bar is hidden, you can display it by going to the "View" menu and selecting the "Show Tab Bar" option.
- After saving the document, the name of the file will appear as the label for the tab.
- You can use keyboard shortcuts to add tabs in specific apps if you have the "Prefer tabs when opening documents" setting in the Desktop & Dock preferences selected. This setting can be found in the preferences. Use the Command-N shortcut when the display mode is set to "In Full Screen" or "Always." To switch to "Never," press Option–Command–N on your keyboard.

Take the following steps on your Mac to manage tabs within an application:

1. You are able to do the following things in an application if it supports tabs:

- Display all of a window's tabs at once: Make sure that "View" is set to "Show All Tabs." To switch to the tab of your choice, click on the tab's name in the tab overview. You can get back to the tab you were working in by selecting "View" > "Exit Tab Overview."

- To move between tabs, click on the one you want to move to. You can also cycle through tabs by using the Control-Tab or Control-Shift-Tab keyboard shortcuts.
- Drag a tab to the left or right to rearrange its position.
- Make a tab behave like a standalone window by doing the following: Either select the tab, navigate to the "Window" menu, and then select "Move Tab to New Window," or you may simply drag the tab so that it moves out of the window.

2. On a Mac, you have the following options for closing tabs within an application:

- Close just one of the tabs: Move your mouse pointer over the tab, and then click the X to close it.
- Close all but one of the tabs: Move the mouse pointer over the tab you want to remain

open, and then press the Option key while clicking the **Close button**.

- In addition, by hitting Command-H or Command-Q, respectively, you can hide or close the application that is now open.

CHAPTER TWELVE

Siri

Siri, Apple's voice assistant, has been flawlessly incorporated into virtually all the company's products, including the Mac. You may easily search for files, modify system settings, and carry out a variety of other operations by using just your voice.

It is possible that you will find it beneficial to enable Siri on your Mac and make use of it, particularly if you are already comfortable with using Siri on your iPhone or iPad. We have included instructions below that will walk you through using Siri on your Mac. Continue reading so that you can discover more possibilities.

What is Siri?

Siri is Apple's digital voice assistant, and it is most widely known for being integrated into the company's mobile products like the iPhone and iPad. Since it was integrated into Mac laptops in 2016, it has received a lot of praise for its usefulness. Siri makes it easier to complete a variety of tasks, including checking the weather, searching for files, adjusting system settings, and more.

You might see a prompt to activate Siri while you are setting up your Mac for the first time or after installing an update to macOS. Within the macOS System Settings, you will find a button that you may click to activate the feature if you have not already done so.

How to enable Siri

Siri can be accessed beginning with macOS Sierra and any subsequent versions of that operating system. Therefore, if your computer is still running macOS 10.11 or an earlier edition, updating to macOS 10.12 or a later version is required in order to activate and make use of Siri on your Mac. This is also the case if you are using an earlier edition of macOS.

Follow the methods that are provided below in order to make Siri work within macOS:

- Launch **System Preferences** on your Mac, and then select **Siri & Spotlight** from the menu on the left.
- To activate Siri, you have to turn on the switch that is labeled "Enable Ask Siri."
- Ask Siri will need to be enabled in order for you to be able to communicate with it using your voice. After this, Siri may ask you to enunciate a few sentences so that it can become familiar with your speech patterns and better understand what you mean when you say things.

Congratulations, the Siri installation on your Mac has been completed without any problems. Additionally, you may modify Siri's voice as well as the language that she speaks in using the same interface. This includes changing the accent that she uses.

How to activate Siri

Once Siri has been enabled on your Mac, you have a number of options available to you for activating it. The phrase "Hey Siri" is the primary method for activating Siri and can be done so by using either your voice or the button on your device. You also have the choice to interact with Siri by pressing the Siri button that is found in the menu bar of your Mac, or you can use the shortcut keys on your keyboard.

The Siri button that is positioned on the Touch Bar of a Mac that is equipped with a Touch Bar can also serve as a quick activation mechanism for users who are using a Mac that is equipped with a Touch Bar. You also have the option of using the "Type to Siri" feature, which enables you to communicate with Siri through the use of text that you have typed in, if you would rather not utilize voice commands.

The following is an explanation of these activation methods:

- **Saying "Hey Siri"**

Utilizing the "Hey Siri" command is the approach that sees the greatest action and usage overall. It is necessary to turn on this feature from under the Siri & Spotlight settings found in the Preferences menu. After being activated, your Mac will be receptive to the "Hey Siri" command, which will cause Siri to be triggered whenever you say "Hey Siri."

During the process of setting up Siri, you will be prompted to say a few sentences so that the software can become familiar with your voice.

After the initial setup is complete, saying "Hey Siri" will cause the Siri window to appear in the top-right corner of the screen. This will give you access to your own personal voice assistant.

- **From the Menu Bar**

You can access Siri by clicking on the Siri button, which is located in the top-right corner of the macOS menu bar. If you do not want Siri to continuously monitor your voice, you can disable this feature. It is located next to the date and offers a simple alternative to the "Hey Siri" command for activating Siri. This shortcut may be accessed by just touching the icon.

- **Making use of Keyboard Shortcuts**

Another choice is to make use of a keyboard shortcut, which, within the context of Siri, refers to the area of System Preferences that allows for its customization. You have the option of using one of the keyboard shortcuts that has been predefined, or you can create your own shortcuts using the

Keyboard Shortcut menu. This configuration enables direct activation of Siri from the keyboard on your Mac.

- **Activation through the Touch Bar**

If you have a MacBook Air with a Touch Bar, the Siri button that is located on the right side of the touch bar provides an extra way to quickly activate Siri. This eliminates the requirement that you reach the Siri button that is located in the menu bar.

- **Option to "Type to Siri"**

The "Type to Siri" feature is there for you to use if you feel more comfortable communicating with Siri through the written word as opposed to voice commands. Within the Accessibility section of System Preferences, you will find the option to activate this feature.

To activate "Type to Siri,"

a. Go to System Preferences > Accessibility and look for the Siri component in the submenu that appears there.

b. Enabling this function gives you the ability to type in commands to Siri, which is useful in situations where vocal communication might not be feasible, such as in public places.

What to use Siri for

You are able to complete a wide variety of things quickly and easily on your Mac with the assistance of Siri, who acts as a multifunctional voice assistant. Supposing that you require assistance identifying files or folders inside the interface of your Mac, a simple inquiry to Siri will launch a quick search. While Spotlight does provide some of these capabilities, using Siri accomplishes the same thing in an equally convenient manner.

You can instruct Siri to look in particular directories if you want to take advantage of its search capabilities when looking through files on your device. Heading towards **System Settings > Siri** is where you'll find the option to make any necessary adjustments to this configuration. You have the flexibility to hand-pick the categories that you want Siri to include in her search results in this section of the settings.

Take, for example, the scenario in which you ask Siri to "retrieve documents generated last week." Siri will immediately give the relevant results after being prompted by your command. In addition to this, Siri is capable of expanding its functionality beyond simple file searches. Siri is capable of performing a wide variety of tasks, including but not limited to providing weather forecasts for the following days, reading your emails, executing Google searches, and more.

The capability to drag and drop items is an invaluable addition to Siri's toolkit. To give you an example, you can give Siri the duty of finding a particular image or file, which will then make it easier for you to attach that item directly to an email message. By using this strategy instead of the standard approach of locating and attaching files using Finder, you will save a significant amount of time.

Using Siri in your Daily Life

After you've gotten Siri set up and running, you should think about how you can incorporate it into your day-to-day activities. By way of illustration, rather than having to launch a separate application, making use of Siri to carry out tasks such as setting reminders or alarms is a more convenient alternative.

The "Hey Siri" voice command is one that the vast majority of users find to be extremely helpful when it comes to activating Siri. On the other hand, you may also activate Siri on your Mac by employing the menu bar, the Touch Bar, or a certain keyboard shortcut. All of these options are available.

CHAPTER THIRTEEN

Security Features built into your Mac

Since the company's inception, Apple has built a solid reputation on the strength of its security measures. However, cybercriminals' attention has been drawn by the meteoric rise in popularity of MacBooks, which has led to a shift in the focus of their attacks toward these devices.

A startling illustration of this pattern can be seen in a study that was conducted in 2021. The study indicated that the production of macOS malware had a meteoric increase of over 1,000 percent in 2020, leading to the disclosure of an astounding count of 674,273 new malware samples.

You will be able to protect the data that is most important to you if you become familiar with the security features of macOS and take the time to learn about them. Keep in mind that the robustness of your protective measures has an inextricable relationship with the safety of the data you save. Devote some of your time to conducting an in-depth analysis of these security features available in macOS so that you can confirm that you are taking all feasible measure to maintain your personal safety in the digital sphere.

Instant Screen Auto-lock

The automatic screen lock is one of the security tools available on your Mac Book air device. Despite its simplicity, it is frequently overlooked. In order to get the most out of this function, you should configure the "Require Password" setting so that it activates "Immediately." This will immediately log you out of your Mac user account, regardless of the length of time that you have been inactive for.

This functionality functions as a precaution in situations in which you might nod off while working at a cafe, obstructing any attempts by persons around to use the information that is available on your screen.

When you need to step away from your Mac in a public situation, or in the terrible case that your Mac is forgotten or stolen, the usefulness of the instant auto-lock becomes immediately apparent, despite the fact that it may initially appear to be a little inconvenient.

The following is the procedure to activate Auto-Lock:

- Simply select the **Apple icon** located in the drop-down menu.
- To access the Security and Privacy settings, go to the **System Preferences menu** first.
- Find the "Require Password" option under the "General" page, and change the setting to "Immediately."

FileVault Encryption

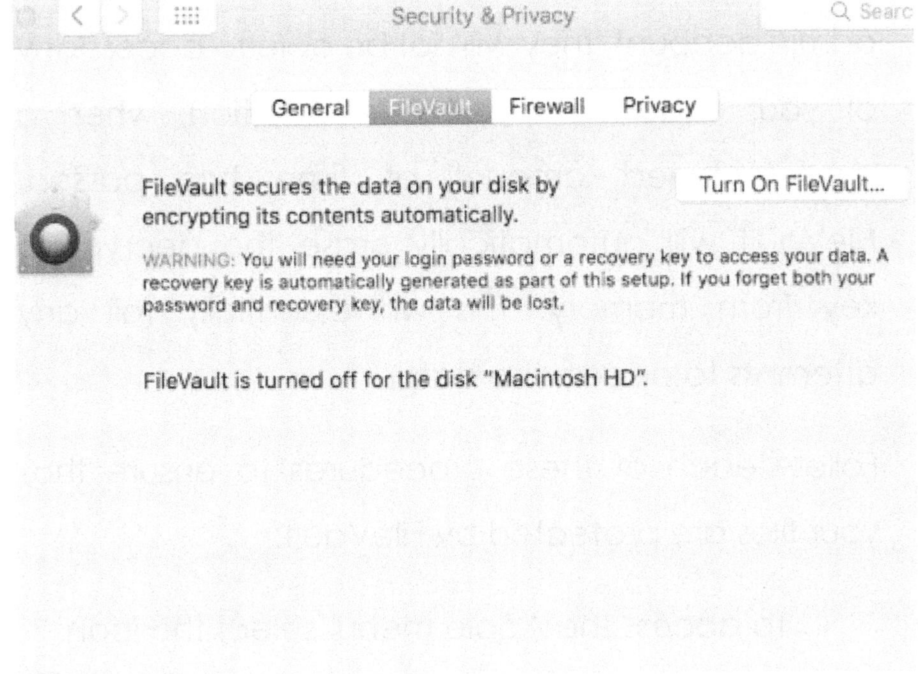

When it comes to the security measures offered by the MacBook Air device, FileVault is considered to be one of the most important components, especially in terms of preventing unauthorized access to your MacBook. Enabling FileVault will result in the encryption of your hard disk, which will make the data stored on it inaccessible to anyone who does not have the specific decryption key.

This indicates that even if a person is successful in figuring out how to overcome the password for your admin account, they will not be able to access any of your important papers. In addition, when a predetermined amount of time has passed, FileVault will automatically erase the decryption key from memory. This will essentially foil any attempts to access the data.

Follow each of these procedures to ensure that your files are protected by FileVault:

- To access the Apple menu, select the icon.
- Go to the **System Preferences menu**, and then select the **Security & Privacy option** from within that menu.
- Click on the tab labeled "FileVault," then click the button labeled "Turn on FileVault."
- After that, you will be given the option to generate a decryption key for the file.

Additionally, we are staunch proponents of extending the FileVault encryption system to cover external disks that are connected to a Mac. Simply attaching an external drive and selecting the "Turn On FileVault" option from the menu will easily accomplish this goal.

Firmware Password

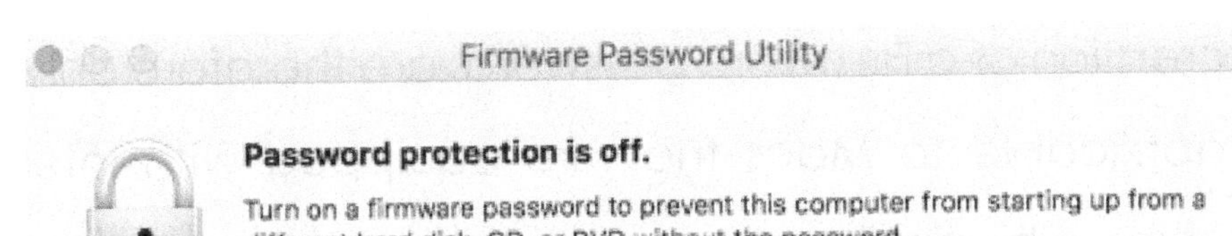

Establishing a firmware password on your Mac system adds an extra degree of safety against cybercriminals who are knowledgeable in technological matters. When you start your Mac in an unusual way, such as booting from an external device, accessing the recovery partition, or using a startup key combination, this safety safeguard requires you to enter a password. If you do not enter a password, your Mac will not start in an unusual way.

On the other hand, it is interesting that Apple's most recent Silicon Macs do not require a firmware password anymore because of an improved technology called FileVault on those computers. The following instructions, which outline the creation of a Firmware password, are therefore only applicable to Macs that are equipped with Intel chips, which still make up the vast majority of Macs that are operational:

Establishing a Password for the Firmware on an Intel Mac:

- In order to use the Firmware Password Utility, you must first power down your Mac to begin the process.
- To access the recovery partition, when the computer restarts, hold down the Command and Return keys simultaneously. This will cause

the computer to boot into the recovery partition.

- Proceed to the Utilities menu: To access the utilities, navigate to that part of the menu.
- To access the firmware password utility, select Startup Security Utility. Pick one of the two options available: the Startup Security Utility or the Firmware Password Utility.
- Activate the Password for the Firmware: When the pop-up box appears, select the option to "Turn on Firmware Password."
- Make Sure It Is a Robust Password: Create a secure password for yourself that is easy to remember yet challenging for others to decipher.
- Reboot your Mac: Finish up by quitting out of all open applications and restarting your Mac from the Apple menu.

It is essential that the significance of strictly following to step 5 be emphasized. The password for the Firmware cannot be readily reset, in contrast to the password for your ordinary admin account. In the case that you forget this password, the only way to get it changed is to go into an Apple shop with a receipt as proof of purchase. Otherwise, you won't be able to access your account.

By according to these rules, you will be able to strengthen the security of your Intel-based Mac, thereby protecting it from potential intrusions caused by unauthorized parties.

Mac Firewall

Your system is protected from prospective attackers or external dangers that are attempting to break through your defenses by means of a firewall, which serves as the principal barrier. It's possible that the fact that most internet routers already have firewall protection built in makes it unnecessary to turn on the firewall on your Mac, but you should rethink that assumption.

When the firewall is disabled, it is much easier to make connections with other Apple devices.

Nevertheless, turning on the firewall on your Mac is still a good idea, especially if you frequently connect to public networks.

Follow these procedures in order to activate the firewall:

- Access the **Security & Privacy section** of System Preferences by navigating to that menu item.
- Make sure the Firewall tab is selected.
- After clicking the lock button, which will allow you to unlock the settings, you will be requested to enter an administrator username and password. These are the same credentials that are used to get into a Mac.
- Continue by selecting the option to "Turn On Firewall" in the drop-down menu.
- Use the Firewall Options to configure the settings to best suit your requirements.
- You have the option to switch to "Stealth Mode," which provides an increased level of protection. Your Mac will not respond to port

scans or connection attempts that originate from unknown sources if you follow these steps. As a result, your Mac will be better able to avoid being discovered by potential hackers.

XProtect Virus Scanner

XProtect is the name of the built-in anti-virus software for Macs, in case you were ignorant of its existence. In order to perform its role, it inspects apps whenever they are updated or launched for the first time, blocking the execution of any potential malware in advance.

The fact that XProtect does not require any kind of manual configuration from the user is a significant plus. It works in the background without drawing attention to itself, but it is always monitoring your safety and doing everything in its power to keep you safe. On the other hand, keeping your operating system up to date is a good precaution to take, and this alone should be sufficient.

On the other hand, XProtect is not completely secure and does have some flaws. According to MacWorld's research, one of its shortcomings is that it is not as effective as specialized third-party software designed specifically for Macs in detecting different types of malicious software.

The Head of Software at Apple, Craig Federighi, admitted in 2021 that "the extent of Mac malware is unacceptable" due to the fact that the recorded occurrences of Mac infections topped those of Windows infections.

Therefore, despite the fact that XProtect does provide some level of protection against malicious software, it is vital to note that its coverage is not as complete as the coverage provided by various third-party Mac anti-malware alternatives that are accessible.

We strongly advise completing in-depth study in order to determine the choice that most closely matches your specifications and preferences. A sensible course of action would be to go for antivirus software that offers a good trade-off between protection and the system's overall performance.

App Sandboxing and Gatekeeper

In addition to Xprotect, macOS has a number of additional helpful security components, such as App Sandboxing and Gatekeeper, which are both essential pieces of macOS' System Integrity Protection (SIP). Both of these features are aligned with Xprotect. These components strengthen Mac systems' defenses against unauthorized programming by working cohesively together.

Sandboxing applications does not offer complete protection against malware; nonetheless, it helps limit the scope of the damage that malware can perform. App Sandboxing places restrictions on programs, prohibiting them from accessing essential folders or files on your Mac. These directories or files could be corrupted by malicious software or other unknown sources, thus it is important to protect them.

On the other side, the Gatekeeper application prevents users of Mac computers from installing software that was created by untrusted sources, thereby protecting them from dangerous malware. This ensures that you may only acquire programs by purchasing them from the App Store or from other developers who have been identified.

In the event that you attempt to install software from unknown sources or software that could potentially contain malware, you will be presented with the following safeguarding notification:

You have the ability to make modifications to the settings of Gatekeeper by following the procedures below:

- First and foremost, access the **System Preferences**.
- Go to the **Security & Privacy menu**, and once you're there, select the **General tab.**

- You have the option of enabling programs to be downloaded from either the "App Store" or the "App Store and Identified Developers." Which option you choose is dependent on your preferences.

Since the release of MacOS Catalina, Gatekeeper has also taken on the job of analyzing applications for the presence of malware and other potential security risks before allowing any application to be run.

Keychain Access Password Manager

It is of the utmost importance to keep your accounts secure, and the use of a powerful and complicated password is one of the most effective precautions that can be taken. However, keeping track of several passwords can be difficult, particularly when it is necessary for each account to have a password that is completely unique.

When faced with a situation like this, the Keychain Access app comes in quite handy.

The program known as Keychain Access functions as a centralized repository for all of your passwords, making them easy to retrieve whenever the occasion calls for it. In addition to this, it keeps track of when your passwords expire, which ensures that you are always using the most recent version.

Keychain Access provides the highest possible level of protection by utilizing the most modern encryption methods available. Each every device has its own unique encryption key, which is used to encrypt the keychain file. This means that even in the extremely unusual event that a keychain file is compromised, unauthorized access to your passwords will continue to be impossible to achieve without the knowledge of the encryption key for your computer.

Keychain Access is the solution for users of Mac computers who are looking for a capable password management solution. The following is a step-by-step instruction on how to access the Keychain Access app:

- Proceed to the **Utilities folder** located inside the **Applications directory** on your computer.
- To open the Keychain Access application, simply double-click on its icon.
- Immediately after launch, you will be presented with a number of 'keychains,' the most visible of which is the Login keychain. After giving your permission for your browser to save passwords for several websites, the passwords for those websites are stored in this repository.
- You also have the option of storing your Keychain in iCloud, which will allow you to access it from a wide variety of devices, including as iPhones, iPads, and other Macs, without any difficulty. The management of your passwords across all platforms will be

much more convenient and flexible as a result of this.

Recording Alerts

With the release of macOS Monterey, users whose computers use Apple's operating system will be notified anytime any application or device attempts to access the user's camera or microphone. This security feature, which will be denoted by an orange dot in the navigation bar, will serve as a vigilant defensive mechanism against any illegal efforts at surveillance.

Mail Privacy Protection

The Mail Privacy Protection feature is a new addition to macOS Monterey. Its purpose is to prevent email senders from tracking the status of your email openings and from determining your location based on your IP address.

Follow these steps to ensure that this feature is turned on and functioning properly on your Mac:

- Begin by opening the **Mail application** on your Mac.
- To access your email, select the "Mail" option from the menu.
- Make sure you select "Preferences."
- To check whether the "Protect Mail Activity" option is activated by default, navigate to the "Privacy" section of the settings menu.

Find My Mac

Find My Mac is the last of your device security features discussed in this chapter, and it is also the most well-known. Find My Mac is a program that was developed expressly for the purpose of catching people who steal Macs. It gives you the ability to track the location of your device, lock it down, and, if required, erase all the information on it.

Find My Mac can be configured in the following manner:

- Begin by opening the **System Preferences**.

- Choose between an Apple ID and an internet account.
- Select **iCloud** from the available alternatives.
- Turn on Find My Mac and give permission to access it.
- You can now keep track of your device by utilizing iCloud.com or the Find My iPhone app on another iOS device. Both of these options are available to you.

You now have access to a full array of your device security capabilities, which allows you to properly protect both your computer and any valuable data stored on it. These tools are at your disposal.

CHAPTER FOURTEEN

Apple MacBook Air Tips and Tricks

No matter if you are a seasoned Mac expert who is constantly eager to learn something new or a total beginner who purchased a Mac for its sleek design but feels bewildered when using it, do not be afraid! We are here to support and direct you through each and every one of the steps in the process. No matter how experienced you are with Apple's Mac, you can rest assured that we have you covered. Join me on this adventure as we work together to ensure that your time spent using a Mac is productive and satisfying. You are not the only one experiencing this, and we are thrilled to be able to assist you in releasing the untapped potential of your device!

In any case, we are hopeful that this list contains at least one piece of advice that will make your day-to-day use of your Mac a little bit more productive.

If you are new to a Mac device and all the features it offers - and there are tons just waiting to be found - we have collected a list of our favorite tips and tricks to help you get the most out of your MacBook. This is true regardless of how long you have used Macs or whether you are new to macOS and all the features it offers.

Thirty-three things you need to know

Here are 33 useful Mac tips that you should already be familiar with.

1. Build a keyboard shortcut for anything

The Mac operating system comes with a number of keyboard shortcuts that have been added by software developers. One example is the ability to access Spotlight by pressing Command and Space Bar simultaneously. However, it is easy to build a shortcut for anything you want within any application. The one and only thing that you will want prior knowledge of is the specific name of the menu command that you wish to add.

- Open **System Settings** by pressing on the ***Apple logo*** in the top left corner of the screen and selecting it from the drop-down menu.
- Once System Settings is open, touch on the Keyboard option to create a keyboard shortcut.
- After that, you will have to go to the 'Keyboard Shortcuts' menu, followed by the 'App Shortcuts' menu.
- You will need to press the plus sign, then choose the program for which you want to make a shortcut, type in the command from the context menu, and then type in the key combination that you want to use for the shortcut.

2. Perform a mass renaming of a collection of files

If you wish to rename a collection of files on a Mac, you can do so relatively easily as long as you are using an operating system that is at least as recent as Yosemite.

- To begin the process of renaming files in bulk, you will first need to choose the files or folders that you wish to modify.
- You can select multiple items by clicking on one, then holding shift while selecting additional items.
- After you have highlighted the group you want to rename, right-click on it and select the 'Rename' option. From the Finder menu, you may also click on the icon that looks like a circle with three dots in the middle of it.
- After that, you'll have the option to Replace Text, Add Text, or Format the names, as appropriate.

3. Take screenshots of the entire page

Taking a screenshot on a Mac is a breeze because to the intuitive interface. You have the option of taking a screenshot of the entire screen or of a selected portion of the screen when you take a screenshot on your computer. After you have taken either one of them, it will save itself to your desktop automatically, and it will display in the bottom right corner of the screen. You can then click on it to annotate it.

You can snap a screenshot of the entire screen by pressing the Shift key, followed by Command, and then 3.

You can take a screenshot of a portion of your screen by pressing the Shift key along with Command and 4, and then drawing a box around the area of the screen that you want to capture.

4. Digitally sign a PDF file via Email

You might think that in order to sign a document, you have to first print it out, then physically sign it, then scan it, and then finally email it back. Thankfully, there is a simpler option. Since it is possible to sign PDFs immediately from within the

Mail app, there is no need to throw away any paper when signing documents.

- You will start by creating a new email in Mail and dragging the PDF that has to be signed into it.
- After that, you will need to move your mouse cursor over it until a tiny arrow button appears in the top right corner.
- You have the option of selecting 'Mark Up' from this menu. After that, the PDF will open, and you will see an option to sign it at the very top; it's the icon that looks like a signature with a cross on the left, and it has a squiggle in the middle.
- You have the option of using a signature that you have already created in the past, or you can make a new signature from scratch. If you want to make a new signature, you have several options: you can draw one on the trackpad of your Mac, you can draw one on your iPhone, or you can write your signature

on a piece of paper and then hold it up to the webcam on your Mac. All of these options are available to you if you make the decision to make a new signature.

5. **Start the Stage Manager program.**

If your Mac is running macOS Ventura, you have access to a function called ***Stage Manager*** that will allow you to rapidly switch between different windows and applications as well as organize all of your open windows and apps.

- You will need to activate Stage Manager by selecting the **Control Center icon** (which looks like two bars with a dot on either side of the bars) in the Stage Manager menu.
- Launch Control Centre, then tap the **Stage Manager tile** in the bottom left corner.
- Once you reach this point, various apps will begin to load on the left side of the screen, while the app you are currently utilizing will

move to the front and center. If you want to utilize two or more apps at the same time, you simply need to drag the other programs onto the app that is currently open. Various windows of the same app will group on top of each other.

6. **Upon login, immediately launch specific applications.**

If there are specific applications that you use on a daily basis and you always start them up, you may configure your Mac to launch those applications immediately after you log in if you always do so. As an illustration, we consistently make use of Mail, Slack, Safari, and Calendar.

- Tap the **Apple symbol** in the top left corner of the screen to open **System Settings**, and then make sure that your account is selected once it's open.
- After that, you'll need to select 'General' and then 'Login Items' from the menu that appears.
- To add an application, you need to touch on the plus sign ('+') and then search the Finder for the program or file that you want to open when you log in.
- To add something to the list, you will first need to select the program or document from the

list, and then you will need to press the "Open" button.

- To quickly add an application to this list, right-click on the icon of the application you want to add, pick 'Options' from the pop-up menu, and then select 'Open at Login' from the submenu that appears.

7. **Use Spotlight for unit conversions**

The spotlight is a wonderful application.

- To bring it up, press **Command** key and the space bar at the same time.
- After that, the search bar will show up, and you can use it to not only look for files, applications, or the answer to a certain inquiry, but also to convert units of measurement and other currencies.
- Simply put anything you wish to convert into the "search" area at the top of the page.

8. **To see all the open windows, use the Mission Control interface.**

You might be shocked by the number of windows and applications that are currently active on your computer at any given time. If you're anything like us, you probably had no idea that you had 15 tabs open in Safari, not to mention Messages, Mail, WhatsApp, Photoshop, and who knows what else.

- Simply pressing the F3 function button will bring up a list of all the windows and applications that you now have open.
- From this list, you will be able to select which one you want to use by tapping on it.

9. **Make your Mac accessible to guests by creating a guest user account**

It is possible to add numerous users to your Mac, which can be useful if multiple individuals in your household use the same computer. This indicates that everyone has the ability to customize their own wallpapers, layouts, preferences, and apps in whatever way they see fit. It is also possible to add a **Guest user**, which will prevent anyone who borrows your Mac from accessing any of your personal papers or files.

- Tap the **Apple logo** in the upper left corner of the screen to access **the System Settings menu**.
- From there, you can add a new user. Click the **Add Account button** after scrolling down to the Users & Groups section.
- To add a Guest user, go to the Add Account screen, press the 'I' button next to Guest User at the top, and then toggle the 'Allow guests to log in to this computer' setting on.

10. Obtain a Wi-Fi password for devices other than your own

Keychain Access is a fantastic feature that comes standard on Apple Mac computers. It will remember practically all of the passwords you use to log in to various websites, including Facebook and Marks & Spencer.

However, it will also remember the passwords for the Wi-Fi networks at each place. However, while your Mac will immediately join a network that it has stored, you may be required to know the Wi-Fi password for another device, such as your phone or tablet.

- You will first need to open up Keychain before you can access any passwords that you have saved, including passwords for Wi-Fi networks.
- To do this as quickly as possible, press Command and Space Bar together and then type in Keychain.
- The password for the Wi-Fi network or website in question can then be viewed by searching for it in the upper-right corner of the screen, selecting Show Password from the menu that appears, and then entering the password for your Mac.

11. Copy and paste without changing the format.

You have the option of copying and pasting from a website or document without bringing over the formatting, which includes things like the font and the size of the font, if you do not want to bring over the formatting. This comes in handy in a variety of situations, such as when you are composing an email and you need to copy something from a webpage.

The text that you want to copy can be copied by selecting it and then pressing Command + C. Press Command Option Shift V to paste the text, and then open the location where you want to paste it, whether it be in Pages, Mail, or somewhere else.

12. Make use of a number of different desktops

You are able to have many desktops open at the same time on a Mac. For instance, you could have

Photoshop or another application open on one desktop while you checked your email on another desktop. By dragging three fingers over your trackpad, you can quickly switch between your several desktops.

- To initiate the creation of a new desktop, you will first need to launch **Mission Control.**
- To accomplish this as quickly as possible, press the F3 key. You will see a '+' in the far right corner of the top bar, which is located above the numerous desktops that you may currently have open. This will allow you to add other desktops.

13. Activate the "Do Not Disturb" setting as soon as possible.

The F6 function key is the quickest way to activate the Do Not Disturb mode, which will suppress any incoming notifications and keep things nice and quiet for a while.

There are other ways to activate Do Not Disturb, which will keep everything nice and quiet for a while. Simply touching it once will turn on the "Do Not Disturb" feature, and tapping it again will turn it off. When it is active, a symbol that looks like a half moon will appear in the navigation bar at the very top of the screen. It is located to the left of the icon that represents the battery.

You can establish a Focus if you want something more granular, in which case you will be able to choose which notifications and apps are allowed to pass through.

- To accomplish this, open the **Control Center** and select **Focus** from the menu that appears in the top left of the screen.
- After that, you can build up a personalized Focus, such as Meeting, by following the directions provided.

14. Use the AirDrop to transfer and share photographs and files.

When it does its job well, AirDrop is an outstanding service. Transferring files and photographs from your iPhone or iPad to your Mac with AirDrop is a fairly fast and simple process, despite the fact that it occasionally experiences some technical difficulties.

- You will need to look for an icon that represents sharing, which is typically a rectangle with an arrow protruding from the top, or you can choose "Share" from the menu of available options.
- After that, you will need to choose AirDrop, and then choose the device that you wish to share with.
- If the device you wish to share with does not appear, open **Finder** on your Mac and pick **AirDrop** from the menu at the top.
- You may be prompted to choose whether you want to be detected by **Contacts Only or**

Everyone. On an iOS device, tap the **Settings icon**, navigate to **the AirDrop menu**, and then select either **Contacts Only or Everyone.**

15. Take a look at your recent notifications.

Your Mac's notifications will flash briefly in the upper right-hand corner of the screen before vanishing unless you hover your mouse pointer over them.

- Tap the date and time in the top right corner of the screen if you want to receive a fast overview of all the notifications that have come through recently, such as emails, Slack messages, Messages alerts, or Find My Phone alerts, for example.
- You will then be presented with a list of your notifications, and you will have the ability to click on any of those alerts to expand it, after which you will be able to take an action from a drop-down menu. You may also bring up

your alerts by swiping across your trackpad with two fingers at the same time.

16. Be sure that your Mac is put to sleep

If you have discovered that your MacBook will not go to sleep even after you have closed the lid or attempted to put it to sleep, there may be an application that is preventing this from happening. There is a technique to check what applications are running in the background on your Mac, which may be delaying it from shutting down. Thankfully, this can be done in a relatively short amount of time.

Spotlight may be used to look for the 'Activity Monitor' app, and the 'Columns' option can be found in the View menu at the very top of the screen. There is a column labeled "Preventing Sleep," and it will indicate that the application in question is a problem by displaying the word "yes" in that column.

17. Hide the Menu Bar

By default, the menu bar will be displayed at the top of the screen on your Mac; however, you have the option to adjust this so that it will only appear when you move your cursor to the very top of the screen. Those users who, for example, prefer not to have any interruptions on their entire screen would benefit from this feature.

- To conceal the menu bar, enter the **System Preferences** by selecting the **Apple icon** located in the upper left corner of the screen.
- After that, you'll need to select 'Desktop & Dock' from the menu at the top of the screen, and then select one of the options from the drop-down menu that's located next to 'Automatically hide and show the menu bar'.

18. Use your mobile device as Wi-Fi hotspot.

If there is no Wi-Fi available but you have cellular coverage on your phone, whether it's an iPhone or another phone, you can connect to the hotspot on your phone in order to access the internet. This works regardless of whether you're using an iPhone or another phone.

- You'll need to know the password for the personal hotspot on your phone, which, on an iPhone, can be found in the Settings app under the Personal Hotspot heading.
- After that, you'll need to navigate to the Wi-Fi icon on your Mac and choose your phone from the drop-down list.
- Then, you'll need to enter the password, and then you should be all set.

It is important to note that you can connect to your iPhone using Bluetooth or USB in order to share its signal.

19. Alter the hot corners

The Mac operating system includes a function known as Hot Corners that gives you the ability to perform quick actions, such as putting your device to sleep, depending on how you have it configured.

- Tap the **Apple logo** located in the top-left corner of the screen to enter **System Settings.**
- Once there, scroll down until you reach the section labeled 'Desktop & Dock' to gain access to the Hot Corners.
- When you click this, you'll see a section called **Hot Corners** at the bottom of the screen. In this section, you can choose what you want your Mac's four corners to do when you move your cursor into those corners.

You could, for instance, set the top left corner to put your Mac to sleep, the top right corner to display application windows, the bottom left corner to open a Quick Note, and the bottom right corner to activate Mission Control.

20. **Split the screen to improve multitasking**

On a Mac, you may, of course, have numerous windows and apps overlapping each other, but you also have the option of using a Split Screen View, just like you can on an iPad, which makes multitasking appear to be in a somewhat more organized fashion. You could, for instance, have Mail open on one side of your screen while creating a document on the other side of your screen. This would enable you to monitor your emails while also working on your assignments.

- To activate the Split Screen View mode, all you have to do is move the pointer over the green icon located in the upper left corner of the program that you wish to display on only one half of your screen.
- There will be a default display of three options: "Enter Full Screen," "Tile Window to Left of Screen," and "Tile Window to Right of Screen."
- After selecting either the left or right choice, you will be given the opportunity to choose a secondary app that will be displayed on the other side of the device.

- To get out of Split Screen View, you need to simply hit the green button that is located in the top left corner of the app that you wish to exit.

21. Modify the icons used for your folders and files

However, if you want to have specific logos or graphics for files rather than the normal preview or blue folder, you have the option to do so with a Mac. The default Mac interface is quite amazing, so you don't need to modify anything about it. And it's not that difficult either.

- To begin, you will need to create the image that you intend to utilize in whichever image editing program is set as your default on your device.
- Select the image you want to copy, then hit the Command key plus the letter C on your keyboard.

- After that, select 'Get Info' from the context menu that appears after you right-click on the file or folder whose icon you wish to modify.
- You can put in your own unique image by selecting the preview image in the upper left corner of the pop-up information card and then pressing the Command and V keys simultaneously.

22. Close any open tabs in Safari on any other Apple devices.

It is possible to close open Safari tabs on other Apple devices signed into your Apple ID using your Mac if you are logged into those devices using your Apple ID. It comes in handy in a variety of situations, such as when you want to ensure that all the tabs on your iPad are closed before giving it to your children.

- To accomplish this, launch Safari and select the cloud icon located to the right of the search box.
- All of the Safari tabs that are currently active across all of your Apple devices will be displayed here.

23. Alter the audio output you are using.

This is a somewhat obvious piece of advice, but one that will undoubtedly come in handy at some point.

- If you want to switch audio between your headphones and your Mac speakers, you will need to tap on the sound icon that is located at the top of your menu bar.
- This is the case if you have headphones attached to your Mac. After that, you will be able to select any headphones that have been attached to your system, in addition to deciding whether or not to use the input device.

24. Enter those unique (and entertaining) characters

When typing, there are a few shortcuts available for accessing the various special characters, such as holding down a character to reveal other alternatives. For instance, if you wanted to type "café," you would have to press and hold the letter "e" in order to access the options that include the accent.

You are also able to type in entertaining characters, such as emoji. You read that correctly; a MacBook Air equipped with a Touch Bar is not required in order for you to be able to enter an emoji. If an app is capable of displaying emojis and symbols, **the Edit menu** will typically include an option labeled "Emoji's & Symbols."

You can also access the other symbols by pressing the ***fn key***, which is located in the bottom left corner of your keyboard. You can search for a specific character symbol by using the search box, or you can filter through different categories by pressing on the rectangular icon that is located in the top right corner of the screen.

25. Make it such that screenshots are saved as JPEG files rather than PNG files.

On a Mac, screenshots that you take are automatically saved in PNG format by Apple; however, this may not always be the best option depending on what you intend to do with the screenshot after you have taken it. You can utilize Terminal to write a block of code in order to alter the type of file that is used by default. Don't freak out; it's not as terrifying as it seems at first glance.

- You can locate Terminal on your Mac by using the Spotlight search.
- After that, you should type "defaults write com.apple.screencapture type JPG" and then hit the enter key on your keyboard. The

effect will occur after you restart your Mac, as soon as you do that.

- If you do not wish to restart, you can avoid doing so by typing "KillAll SystemUIServer" and then pressing the enter key.
- You will need to type "defaults write com.apple.screencapture type PNG" and hit enter to revert back to PNG. After that, you will need to either restart your computer or press "KillAll SystemUIServer" and hit enter.

26. **Copying links in a flash**

Simply pressing Command + L, then Command + C will allow you to copy a link in Safari in a flash. It will highlight the full link at once, which is a far faster alternative than manually dragging your cursor to the end of the link.

27. **Communicate with Siri**

Siri was around for quite some time before other digital assistants like Alexa, and it also has a witty side. You may use Siri for a variety of purposes, like setting reminders and alarms, in addition to asking it questions about a wide range of topics.

Simply click the icon that represents Siri at the very top of your menu bar to begin chatting with Siri on your Mac.

28. **Navigate between the various apps.**

This is a favorite of ours. When it comes to switching between apps, it's not complicated at all, but it does its job really well. Simply pressing the **Command key** along with the Tab key will bring up the Application Switcher.

- First you'll need to keep Command pressed, and after that, you'll be able to move between apps by pressing Tab.
- As soon as the application you wish to launch is highlighted, you can release Command and Tab, and the app will launch.

29. Use your Apple Watch to unlock.

If you have an Apple Watch and a Mac, you can configure your Mac so that it will unlock automatically whenever you put on your Apple Watch. It saves you from having to put in your password, but if you have a more recent Mac with Touch ID incorporated into the keyboard, unlocking your Mac is relatively rapid regardless of whether or not this feature is available to you.

- To configure an Apple Watch for automatic unlocking, enter **System Settings** by tapping on the **Apple icon** located in the upper left corner of the display and selecting it from the menu that appears.
- After that, you will need to navigate to the 'Touch ID & Password' menu and activate your Apple Watch from the available options there.

30. Immediately start recording your screen.

Even if we've covered how to take a screenshot and how to take a screenshot of the entire screen, it's still possible to rapidly capture your screen. You need to press the Command key together with the number 5.

31. Exit the application using the App Switcher.

It's possible that when you launch App Switcher, you'll discover that you have many more apps open than you originally assumed.

- If you wish to leave an application while it is highlighted in App Switcher, all you have to do is press the 'Q' key on your keyboard. This will allow you to close the application.

32. Make use of various mouse and trackpad gestures

You can gain immediate access to a variety of Mac capabilities by utilizing a selection of gestures that can be performed on the Trackpad and Mouse. The challenge is to commit all of them to memory. Some of our favorites include swiping leftward with two fingers to activate the notification center, clicking with two fingers to execute a right click, and pinching with two fingers to zoom in or out of an image. There are a lot of them, though, such as spreading your thumb and three fingers apart to display your desktop and swiping up with four fingers to open Mission Control.

33. Use the Universal Clipboard to copy and paste between devices

You are able to copy text, graphics, photos, and videos from one Apple device, such as your iPhone, and then paste it on another Apple device, such as your Mac.

Universal Clipboard is a feature that is exclusive to Apple products. Both devices require that you are signed in with the same Apple ID, that Bluetooth and Wi-Fi are turned on, and that Handoff is activated before they may communicate with one another.

After you've taken care of that, all that's left to do is copy something on the first device and then paste it as you normally would on your Mac.

CHAPTER FIFTEEN

Troubleshooting

In this chapter, we will discuss typical issues that owners of the MacBook Air may come across and offer efficient strategies for resolving those issues. It is imperative that a basic understanding of the MacBook Air be attained before digging into the aforementioned problems and the solutions to them.

The MacBook Air changed the portable computing industry with its thin profile, which measured only 1.94 centimeters in thickness. Even though it has a sleek look and is convenient to use, the MacBook Air, just like any other electronic product, can have problems that require troubleshooting.

We will investigate common difficulties such as failure to power on, unexpected shutdowns, flashing question marks during startup, and black screen issues, as well as the remedies to these problems. All the many models of the MacBook Air are compatible with these solutions.

Common MacBook Air Problems and solutions

1. **The first problem is that the MacBook Air would not turn on**

If you try to turn on your MacBook Air and it does not react, you may need to try restarting it. This problem typically occurs as a result of faulty booting or crashes in the system. The following is an in-depth walkthrough of how to diagnose and fix this issue, step by step:

Solution: Check the RAM

If you power up your MacBook Air and hear three beeps, followed by a black screen, and then the computer shuts down, the RAM may be to blame. In the unfortunate event that the RAM is faulty, the logic board or possibly even the entire motherboard will need to be replaced. Because the RAM is soldered directly onto the logic board, the only way to fix this problem is to replace the board in its whole.

Solution: Power Supply Adapter in Need of Repair

Your inability to start up your MacBook Air may be the result of a faulty power adaptor. Your device will not charge if the power adapter is not working properly, which can result in a depleted battery as well as unexpected power-offs while it is being used. An angled connector is featured on the customized adapter that comes standard with every MacBook Air. Verify that the battery has an adequate charge before attempting to troubleshoot a broken power adapter. Borrow a battery or power adapter that works if you need to in order to determine whether or not the adapter is the source of the problem. If the issue continues, it is likely connected to the logic board or the motherboard, and one of those components will need to be replaced.

Solution: Problem with Thermal Sensors

It's also possible that the temperature sensor on your MacBook Air is broken, which would prevent it from turning on. Despite the fact that the laptop is unable to boot, there are indications that include abnormally high fan RPMs. This circumstance indicates that the thermal sensor is not working properly. Because thermal sensors are built into the logic board and the motherboard, either one of these components will need to be replaced in order to solve this issue.

Solution: The faulty logic board

If you've already tried those solutions, but the problem persists, it's possible that the problem lies with the logic board. This is especially likely to be the case if your MacBook Air starts up with nine consecutive beeps. You are going to need to switch out the logic board on the MacBook Air in order to fix this significant issue.

2. **When the charger is removed, the MacBook Air automatically powers off**

Even with a fully charged battery, one of the most prevalent problems encountered by owners of the MacBook Air is an unexpected shut down that occurs when the charger is disconnected. There are a few potential causes and solutions to investigate if you are having issues with your MacBook Air turning off after you have unplugged the charger from it.

Battery Failure:

The rapid shutdown was most likely caused by a faulty or dead battery. This is the most plausible explanation. When the laptop's battery is unable to maintain a charge, the device must rely solely on its accompanying power adapter. Check for the following symptoms to determine whether or not this is the cause of the problem:

- The battery does not charge at all (although it is possible that the problem lies with the logic board).
- The laptop either does not recognize the battery's presence or displays that it is fully charged even though it is unable to run on battery power.

Solution: It is going to be necessary for you to switch out the battery in your MacBook Air in order to fix this issue. For assistance, you should get in touch with a qualified specialist.

Problems with the Software:

In certain instances, the issue may not be with the battery itself but rather with the power management settings of the system or with software-related issues.

Solution: If you're having problems with the power supply on your MacBook Air, you should try to reset the System Management Controller, often known as the SMC. In order to accomplish this, please follow these steps:

- Exit all applications on your MacBook Air.
- Make sure the power adapter is connected.
- While simultaneously pressing and holding the Shift, Control, and Option keys, as well as the power button, for approximately ten seconds.
- Let go of all the keys, including the button for the power.
- Continue using your MacBook Air as you normally would.

Problems with the Hardware

There is a possibility that there is a problem with the hardware, such as a malfunctioning power circuitry, a loose connection, or problems with the charging port.

In the event that the problem is not fixed by following the instructions outlined above, the best course of action is to seek assistance from a qualified technician or an authorized Apple service provider. They are able to diagnose and correct any problems that are caused by the underlying hardware.

In summary, if your MacBook Air goes off when the charger is disconnected, the problem is most likely caused by a dead battery or problems relating to either the software or the hardware. First, verify the condition of the battery, and then think about resetting the system management controller. If the issue continues, you should seek the advice of a specialist who can adequately identify and address the underlying source of the problem.

3. MacBook Air Displays a Flashing Question on Startup

The problem of a blinking question mark folder that shows on the screen of your MacBook Air during startup is going to be the topic of discussion in the following paragraphs. This section will walk you through the process of fixing one of the most prevalent issues with a MacBook Air, which is a flashing question mark on startup error.

When you turn on your Mac, if a flashing question mark shows on the startup screen, here is what you need to know to comprehend it. When the computer is unable to locate an operating system that is capable of being booted, it starts up with a blinking question mark. It is possible that one of the following is to blame for this issue: either your operating system is damaged, your laptop does not have enough RAM, or your hard disk is failing. The following is a list of the procedures that need to be taken in order to fix an error on a Mac that displays a flashing question mark.

- **Bad Operating System**

When you turn on your MacBook Air, you may notice that it displays a blinking question mark throughout the startup process. One of the most common reasons for this problem is a malfunctioning operating system. In this instance, the problem can be fixed by first attempting to boot from an operating system CD. Launch Apple's Disk Utility and check for any errors or problems with the disk. If this does not work, then you will have to reinstall the operating system on your computer. Erase everything on the hard disk before trying to reinstall the operating system if you can.

- **Not Sufficient in RAM**

This problem is extremely uncommon, but the blinking question mark can appear on your screen if your computer does not have enough random access memory (RAM) to successfully load the operating system. To fix this issue, you will need to either upgrade the amount of RAM in your PC or switch to an operating system that is many versions older. RAM requirements increase from 512 megabytes for OS X 10.5 to 1 gigabyte for OS X 10.6.

- **Problematic hard drive**

When this happens, the hard disk on the laptop may have been accidentally deleted, corrupted, or destroyed, which causes the flashing question mark error to appear while the laptop is loading up. In order to resolve this issue, you will need to complete the actions that are listed below. If the data on the hard drive has been deleted, you will first need to reinstall your operating system and format the drive using the HFS+ file system. Should the data on the hard drive get corrupted, you will be need to replace it.

Hard disks that are on their way out may exhibit sporadic instances of data corruption before giving up completely. In addition, they frequently become more audible with time and begin to click. Therefore, if your hard drive is producing strange clicking noises but is still operational, you should immediately replace the hard drive and make sure that a backup of your data is created before the drive fully fails.

4. **Problems with the unresponsiveness and black screen of the MacBook Air**

An issue on your MacBook Air that results in a black screen, sometimes known as the "Black Screen of Death," can cause you to feel frustrated and confused. Because of this issue, your device may become unresponsive, which will interfere with your workflow. In this tutorial, we will investigate the factors that led to the occurrence of this issue and present workable options for addressing it.

I. Localizing the Source of the Problem

The "black screen" error that occurs on a MacBook Air typically results from problems with the display or the logic board. To effectively troubleshoot a problem, it is essential to have a solid understanding of these factors.

II. Solving Issues That Are Associated With Displays

- **Changing the Display**

If the black screen is the result of a faulty display, you might think about switching it out for a unit that is compatible with your device. Following these detailed instructions will assist in restoring the correct visual functionality to your MacBook Air.

- **Replace the Logic Board**

In the event that changing the display does not resolve the issue, it is possible that the problem lies with the logic board. To resolve issues with a black screen that won't go away, familiarize yourself with the process of replacing the logic board.

III. Fixing Problems with Bluetooth and AirPort Connectivity on a MacBook Air

Issues with your ability to connect to Bluetooth and AirPort can detract from your overall wireless experience. In order to successfully diagnose and solve these problems, follow these procedures in order.

- **Problems with Bluetooth and AirPort May Cause These Symptoms**:

Recognize the common symptoms, such as icons that are grayed out, error messages, and the absence of functionality related to AirPort.

- **Identifying the Problem and Repairing the Loose Connector Cable:**

Problems with Bluetooth and AirPort connections are commonly caused by unsecured connector cables. The following is a diagnostic and repair procedure for this issue:

a. Detach the MacBook's lower casing from the device.
b. Inspect the connection of the cable to the logic board; if it seems a little sloppy, give it a light press until you hear it click firmly into place.
c. Check that the connector on the wireless board is likewise correctly attached before moving on.
d. Put the MacBook back together by reattaching the lid to the bottom of the device.

5. MacBook Air: Additional Issues and How to Fix Them

Ports/Audio

Another issue that is extremely widespread with the MacBook Air is one that pertains to its audio and ports. There can be occasions when you discover that the sound system on your laptop is not functioning properly or that it is deteriorating. If the built-in speakers on your Mac are not producing any sound, you will need to seek assistance in this situation. In this post, we will explore what to do if the sound on your MacBook is not working and how to fix it. Additionally, we will cover what to do if there is no sound on your Mac.

The simple solution to this widespread audio issue on Mac can be found below. Problems with the audio on a Mac can occur if the computer's USB ports or audio ports stop working properly. Nevertheless, these ports are located on a distinct portion of the logic board. Therefore, in order to resolve this issue, you will need to replace the assembly of the port hatch.

It is essential that you keep in mind the following: if you are unable to use another component of your computer, such as the display, the battery, or even the electricity, and replacing the component that did not appear to be functioning properly did not resolve the issue, it is probable that the logic board will need to be replaced.

CONCLUSION

In conclusion, the Apple MacBook Air 15-inch (2023) stands out as a genuine paradigm shifter, pushing both design and performance standards simultaneously. It emerges as the ideal companion for professionals and students who require a trustworthy mobile workstation since it comes equipped with a dazzling Retina display, a strong M2 CPU, and an amazing battery lifespan. These three features make it a competitive contender.

The investment in this laptop is undoubtedly rewarded despite the fact that it comes with a premium price tag, given the exceptional features that it brings to the table that are not found in any other laptop.

Taking everything into consideration, the Apple MacBook Air 15-inch (2023) is, without a shadow of a doubt, one of the best options you can go with if you're looking for a portable computer that is not only roomy and powerful but also smoothly integrates cutting-edge technology with an unrivaled level of portability.

ABOUT THE AUTHOR

Perry Hoover is a researcher, tech Entrepreneur, blogger and a technology writer, who is fond of blogging, technology research and writing. His areas of interest include Web application penetration testing, web security/architecture, cryptography, programming languages and database security. He is well versed with the latest technology, programming languages, computer hardware/software, and programming tools. He is also an expert in database security and application security architecture and penetration testing. He loves to share information about new technology and has published dozens of articles on it.

He has written articles on different aspects of IT Technologies including IT security, data storage and application development for magazines and has also published and co-published several e-books, of which the latest is on Windows 11. He has also worked with different private agencies to provide solutions to IT problems.

Made in the USA
Middletown, DE
27 January 2024

48632986R00149